Hiking through History:
Civil War Sites on the Appalachian Trail

Hiking through History:
Civil War Sites on the Appalachian Trail

Including the Underground Railroad and the Brown Mountain Creek Freedmen Settlement

Leanna Joyner

APPALACHIAN TRAIL CONSERVANCY®

Harpers Ferry

Published by the Appalachian Trail Conservancy, 799 Washington Street, Harpers Ferry, West Virginia 25425-0807.

ISBN 978-1-889386-94-2

First edition. Printed in the United States of America.

Maps by Paul Lobue of Mapping Specialists, Ltd., Fitchburg, Wisconsin
Design by David T. Gilbert

Front cover: Map of South Mountain showing the positions of Confederate and Union forces on September 14, 1862. United States Army Corps of Topographical Engineers, N.Y., Photolitographic Co. (Osborne's process), 1872. (Library of Congress Geography and Map Division)

Back cover: The graves of Daniel Shelton, William Shelton, and Millard Haire along the Appalachian Trail in North Carolina. (Photo by Leanna Joyner)

Dedicated to the Trail pioneers and volunteers, and our governmental partners, who for almost a century have helped preserve these sites and perhaps the spirits within, as an accessible piece of Americana.

Contents

Foreword

Imagine walking along the ridges of South Mountain in the most narrow, central part of Maryland—the snippet between West Virginia and Pennsylvania—and coming across alongside an old stone fence a young man of about 25, a bit thin at 140 pounds for his five-foot-eight frame, a little scruffy in his attire, carrying what he needs to survive on his back and in his hands.

Today, that might be an Appalachian Trail thru-hiker taking a break within this thick, second-growth forest. And, "survive" would be too strong a word—a town where he could resupply is just a relatively short walk and a hitch-hike away. Only natural sounds suffuse these woods. He has about a 28 percent chance of completing his thru-hike and returning home. Perhaps he would not be thinking about what happened here in the middle of the nineteenth century or the tangible remains of history buried beneath his feet, captured in the soil or the roots of these towering trees. We want to change that.

In 1862, he would be the common soldier of the United States' Civil War, and "survive" might be too polite a word. The sounds he hears are the heralds of the gates of hell, the audio version of the Book of Revelation.

Had he been a Rebel looking for cover for the battle he knows is coming, he had about a 12.5 percent chance of dying in combat this day or a 20 percent chance of dying from disease next week. He had as much chance of being captured as he did of living to make it home, mostly likely to a farm. Were he fighting for the Union, working his way west up the slope, he had a five or six percent chance of being killed in battle, a 10 percent chance of being captured, or a 12.5 chance of being killed by illness. If he were black, he had a twenty percent chance of losing his life.

In a matter of a few days in 1862, along a two-mile stretch of the current Appalachian Trail on South Mountain, hundreds of young men perished under fire. Thousands of them would leave those rocks and gullies and perish two days later on either side of Antietam Creek outside the still-sleepy town of Sharpsburg.

During the Civil War of April 1861 to April 1865, an estimated 620,000 to 750,000 Americans died in battle or from military-related disease—including, in the conventional estimate, 50,000 civilians. That human catastrophe is equal to all American casualties in *all* its military conflicts combined, from the Revolution to either sometime during the Vietnam war (by the older conventional estimate) or until this day (by the more recent analysis).

An estimated one in three households in the South suffered at least one death; many, especially in the South, never learned where their loved one was hastily buried as the army moved along to the next clash. One in four soldiers never returned home. Of those in uniform who lived, an estimated one in thirteen came home missing a limb, to a flattened economy and shredded social fabric. This war inaugurated the concept of national cemeteries. "Veterans benefits" were still a policy of a far future. Record-keeping was less than meticulous.

A small part of that national devastation played out along the ridges and valleys that now are home to the Appalachian Trail, a route that has been a thread through American history for four centuries, back to its days as the frontier populated by a few hardy mountain settlers.

We publish this book to memorialize that history, now conjoined with our Trail's.

This route in the decades preceding that unmatched national bloodshed also occasionally served as a route to freedom for the few among the four million slaves who managed to escape the shackles. No doubt not a few also died along this route; no one knows. Whatever rationales the common soldier may have conjured as a reason to serve and serve valiantly, the secession documents and speeches and writings of the Confederate elite are unequivocal in stating that this rebellion sought to maintain slavery—and the economic infrastructure that benefitted Northerners as well.

And so we determined that this book should memorialize as well the trail's historical connections to the Underground Railroad and to the new lives some freed slaves found along its permanent corridor.

We can only hope that hikers walking through the sites named here, from North Carolina into central Pennsylvania, will entertain at least a passing thought about the skirmishes and battles that happened in these regenerated woods, the blood captured deep in this ground—and give a passing nod of respect to the spirits of those from the 1800s who here sought freedom, fought against perceived aggression, or battled insurrection with the intensity of someone who knows he might die in the next hour.

—*Brian B. King*

Moving Toward Freedom

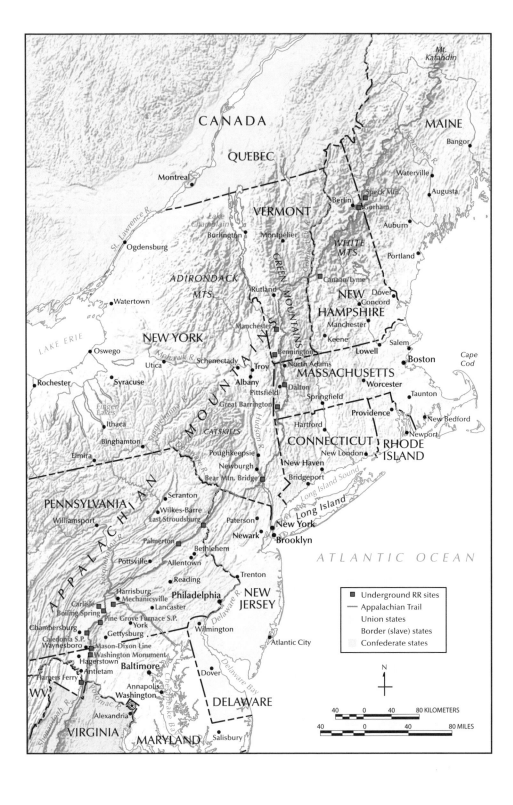

CANADA

QUEBEC

Montreal

MAINE

Mt. Katahdin

Bangor

Waterville

Augusta

VERMONT

Berlin

Speck Mtn.
Gorham

Auburn

Ogdensburg

Lake Champlain

Burlington

Montpelier

Portland

WHITE MTS.

NEW HAMPSHIRE

ADIRONDACK MTS.

Watertown

Rutland

Canaan/Lyme

Dover
Concord

Manchester

Manchester

Keene

Salem

LAKE ERIE

NEW YORK

Oswego

GREEN MOUNTAINS

Bennington

Lowell

Boston

Cape Cod

Mohawk R.

Schenectady

Troy

North Adams

MASSACHUSETTS

Utica

Albany

Worcester

Rochester

Syracuse

Pittsfield

Dalton

Springfield

Taunton

Finger Lakes

Ithaca

Great Barrington

Hartford

Providence

New Bedford

CATSKILLS

Binghamton

Poughkeepsie

CONNECTICUT

New London

Newport

RHODE ISLAND

Elmira

Hudson R.

Newburgh

New Haven

Bear Mtn. Bridge

Bridgeport

Long Island Sound

APPALACHIAN MOUNTAINS

Scranton

Paterson

New York

Long Island

Wilkes-Barre

East Stroudsburg

Newark

Brooklyn

ATLANTIC OCEAN

PENNSYLVANIA

Williamsport

Palmerton

Bethlehem

Susquehanna R.

Pottsville

Allentown

Reading

Trenton

Harrisburg
Mechanicsville

Philadelphia

NEW JERSEY

Carlisle
Boiling Spring

Lancaster

Pine Grove Furnace S.P.

York

Chambersburg

Gettysburg

Wilmington

Atlantic City

Caledonia S.P.
Waynesboro

Mason-Dixon Line

Washington Monument

Delaware R.

Hagerstown

Baltimore

Delaware Bay

WV

Harpers Ferry

Antietam

Washington

Annapolis

Dover

Chesapeake Bay

Alexandria

DELAWARE

Potomac R.

VIRGINIA

Shenandoah R.

MARYLAND

Salisbury

N

■ Underground RR sites
— Appalachian Trail
  Union states
  Border (slave) states
  Confederate states

40   0   40   80 KILOMETERS

40   0   40   80 MILES

The path of the Underground Railroad

The Appalachian Trail is a place for movement and migration—now and as its then-unnamed and happenstance route may have been in the past, well more than 150 years ago.

Hikers on the Appalachian Trail now pass specific Underground Railroad locations. It is difficult to precisely identify when the Underground Railroad began, but evidence that slaves were escaping from bondage as early as the colonial era has been recorded.[1] What documents exist do indicate that the network of escape routes—originating at the point of enslavement but fanning out in all directions possible—became more organized and embedded in the culture following the 1850 Fugitive Slave Act and its abuses. Those who have studied the route and destinations of the Underground Railroad say they were neither standard nor singular, so it is somewhat difficult to identify with certainty routes that are laid out as clearly as the Appalachian Trail is today. The routes followed natural "channels" and created transportation paths on land and water. Runaway slaves on their own, or with the assistance of Underground Railroad "conductors," in order to safely make it to freedom made daily decisions that changed the course of their journeys. Some traveled by coastal routes as stowaways headed toward northern ports. Others chose a land route and may have fled on foot through swamps or navigated beyond the Piedmont and foothills into the mountains, all the while headed north or west or northwest.

Freedom for many lay in Canada, because a British law passed in 1834 abolished slavery throughout the British Empire. Northern and other free states were also the destination of many freedom-seekers, although, after the Fugitive Slave Act of 1850, it became more important than ever for men and women to make it all the way to Canada or another country.

The Underground Railroad was a tangled web of routes and potential routes. It was varied and mysterious, sometimes documented and preserved for our knowledge, but, in other instances, the paths are saved in folklore but lost to history and known only in the hearts of those who escaped along their paths to freedom.

The Appalachian Trail overlaps with the known Underground Railroad primarily north of Harpers Ferry, along South Mountain in Maryland and at sites in the Cumberland Valley in Pennsylvania.

Little other documentation provides details of a specific Appalachian route or stops along the ridges from northern Georgia through North Carolina, Tennessee, and Virginia. Repeated evidence in John Brown's belongings (and among his followers') suggests that the Appalachian Range extending south into the Carolinas and Georgia offered an established, if individually adapted, path offering a "rugged, lonely, but comparatively safe route to freedom." [2]

The mountains served as a guide as well as a path. The Appalachian range "marked the direction to be taken." Just as the North Star and moss on the north side of trees was an indication of the direction of travel, so, too, was the distant range lying south to north—pointing the way. [3]

It is known that African-Americans seeking freedom from slavery walked the flanks of South Mountain in Maryland on a route north to Pennsylvania. [4] Once in Pennsylvania, several locations along the A.T.'s current path offered a place to stay and rest before the escape continued. Those places include confirmed locations at Caledonia Iron Works and Boiling Springs and speculative locations at Pine Grove Furnace and Boiling Springs.

In Maryland

The ridge of South Mountain through Maryland is purported to have been an old Indian trail that escaped slaves used *en route* to freedom. [5] However, the Potomac Appalachian Trail Club denies that a continuous trail along the crest of South Mountain existed when the route was laid out and built for the Appalachian Trail in 1931–1932. [6]

While a walk along the ridgetop of South Mountain may have carried fugitive slaves to freedom, stronger evidence supports their travel along the flanks of South Mountain, both on the western and eastern sides. [7]

In the trail town of Boonsboro below the ridge, for example, escaped slaves found refuge on their way north to Mechanicsburg, Pennsylvania. [8]

Freedom-seekers walking any portion of South Mountain were exposed. The ridge was cleared of most of its vegetation back then. Trees had been cut and burned in hearths to create the charcoal to heat the numerous iron furnaces in the area. Movement must have been stealthy and swift.

In Pennsylvania

Crossing the century-old Mason-Dixon line into Pennsylvania may have felt like a victory for on-the-run slaves, but their freedom was not truly secured until they reached Canada. In border states, such as Pennsylvania, it was too lucrative for slave-catchers to claim blacks as found property and return them to Southern slaveholders, particularly after the Fugitive Slave Act of 1850.

At the Mason-Dixon line, towns on either side of what is now the A.T. were places where freedom-seekers could stop over with "conductors," although they may have preferred to continue north on their own rather than stop. Rouzerville, fewer than two miles west of the A.T., and Blue Ridge Summit, about a mile to the east of the Trail, are documented locations of Underground Railroad stations.[9]

Whether receiving assistance from others or arriving on their own, those traveling the South Mountain route out of Maryland were likely heading initially to places such as Caledonia and Pine Grove Furnace.[10] According to the Journey Through Hallowed Ground Partnership, furnaces were often havens for freedom-seekers.[11]

Caledonia Iron Works

Thaddeus Stevens, a successful lawyer, abolitionist, and politician, built Caledonia Iron Works (now Caledonia State Park) in partnership with James Paxton in 1837. Named for the county of Stevens' birth in Vermont, the furnace—drawing on the hundreds of acres of nearby woods—employed freed or fugitive blacks and was operated by people sympathetic to the antislavery cause. The facility, under the guidance of Superintendent William Hammett, served as an Underground Railroad stop between Maryland and points north. In addition to providing shelter and aid for fugitive slaves, the furnace gave them an opportunity to earn money.

The iron works at both Caledonia and Pine Grove Furnace were also little villages, the former on sites that are now just a short walk east of the northbound A.T. after it crosses U.S. 30 in Pennsylvania's Caledonia State Forest. Blacksmiths, stores, grist mills, and homes where the workers lived all comprised the communities.

According to William J. Switala in *The Underground Railroad in Pennsylvania*, fugitive slaves arriving from Maryland would trek to "Africa," a small African-American community near Caledonia Iron Works, which employed some residents. The next segment of their journey was through a wooded region that has since become Michaux State Forest, and their next destination would have been Pine Grove Furnace.[12]

His description sounds strikingly similar to the path of the Appalachian Trail today.

Thaddeus Stevens was a lawyer, a statesman, an abolitionist, a gambler, and an entrepreneur. His public life is intertwined with the Underground Railroad, the iron industry, the Civil War, and Reconstruction. The Appalachian Trail route crosses paths with Stevens' rich history on several occasions.

As a lawyer, Stevens represented blacks as well as those prosecuted for assisting runaway slaves. In 1849, along with several other defense attorneys, Stevens argued the case for Daniel Kaufman of Boiling Springs, Pennsylvania, who was eventually found guilty and fined for the assistance he provided fugitive slaves.

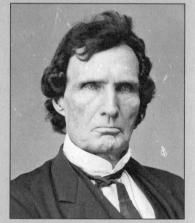

As a politician, Stevens advocated for public schools while he was a representative in the Pennsylvania House.[23] He also fought for the right for black males to vote, although that was an argument he did not win.[24]

Later, in Congress as a leading Radical Republican, he fought for equal rights for immigrants and women as a U.S. representative from Pennsylvania, in time becoming the effective, if not titular, leader of the House.[25] Additionally, after the Civil War, he wrote

Thaddeus Stevens (Library of Congress)

and pushed for ratification of the 13th and 14th amendments to the Constitution, which abolished slavery and established equal rights (other than suffrage for women) and due process for all people, respectively.[26] (It would take a separate amendment in the next century to provide suffrage for women.)

Stevens' most prominent contribution to the story of the Appalachian Trail's sites related to the Civil War, however, is the Caledonia Iron Works (what is now Caledonia State Park). The iron works, financed by Stevens and James Paxton, opened in 1837. The iron-smelting facility employed free blacks in the production of metal.

Underground Railroad researchers have identified Caledonia as a destination for freedom-seekers, who received assistance from William Hammett, the furnace foreman,[27] or from any number of freed blacks living in the nearby community of "Africa."[28]

Thaddeus Stevens was also an Underground Railroad "conductor," helping runaway slaves when he lived in Gettysburg and later in Lancaster.[29]

Just prior to the Battle of Gettysburg on June 23, 1863, in an effort to stem the flow of iron for weapons production for the North as much as to personally protest Steven's vocal and unwavering feelings on abolition, Confederate General Jubal A. Early, in a foray into Pennsylvania days before Gettysburg, ordered Caledonia Iron Works burned. This casualty of the war was of great expense to Stevens.

As recounted in a *Guide to the Appalachian Trail in Pennsylvania*, Stevens detailed his losses in a letter on July 11:

> "[The rebels] took all my horses, mules, and harness, even the crippled horses that were running at large. They then seized my bacon (about 4,000 lbs.), molasses and other contents of the store—took about $1,000 worth of corn in the mills, and a like quantity of other grain. On Friday, they burned the furnace, sawmill, two forges and a rolling mill. They slept in the office and storeroom on that night and burnt them with books and all on Saturday morning.

> "They even hauled off my bar iron, being as they said convenient for shoeing horses and wagons about $4,000 worth. They destroyed all my fences (I had just built a large quantity of post and rail fences, as I was cleaning out a farm.) My grass (about 80 tons) they destroyed; and broke in the windows of the dwelling houses where the workmen lived. They could not have done the job much cleaner. It is rather worse than I expected. All the bellows and bellows houses and run-out establishments are gone." [30]

Stevens did rebuild the furnace in 1865, incurring heavy debt to do so. Sponsor of the resolution to impeach President Andrew Johnson and chairman of the committee drafting the articles of impeachment, he died in Washington in 1868.[31]

Stevens advocated racial equality in Congress, defended it in courts, and personally hosted fugitives on the Underground Railroad in his home. Visitors wanting to pay homage to Stevens will find him laid to rest in Lancaster, Pennsylvania, at Schreiner-Concord Cemetery, one that allowed both blacks and whites to be interred. As he desired, his gravestone reads: "I repose in this quiet and secluded spot…that I might illustrate in my death the principles which I advocated through a long life, equality of man before his Creator."

~

The scant 13 miles between Caledonia Iron Works east to Gettysburg also was a route for slaves on their way to Harrisburg. Thaddeus Stevens and as many as six others in Gettysburg hosted self-liberators arriving from Caledonia or other points south.[13]

Caledonia State Park Hike

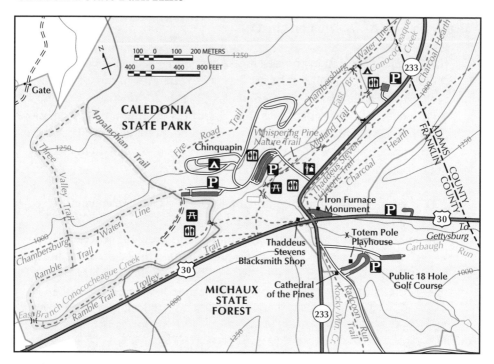

Distance: 1.45 miles
Difficulty: Easy
Trailhead parking: Arrive at Caledonia State Park by taking the exit for U.S. 30 off I-81. Travel east on U.S. 30 for 10 miles. At the intersection with Pa. 233, turn left, passing a parking area on your right at an iron-furnace monument. Continue on Pa. 233 another 0.1 mile. The entrance to the park is on your left. Beyond the ranger station and information center, the road passes one parking lot on the left and continues past the entrance to Chinquapin Hill camping area near the swimming pool. The trailhead parking lot is the *next* left.
Description: From the trailhead parking lot, the Appalachian Trail passes just beyond the picnic tables of this day-use area. Proceed on the Appalachian Trail south toward the playground and in the direction of U.S. 30. The Trail parallels Conococheague Creek for a short distance and intersects with the Ramble Trail. Rather than proceed on the A.T. farther south across U.S. 30, take the right fork of the junction, and continue to parallel the creek, crossing over two small bridges. The Ramble Trail intersects the Three Valley

Trail, and hikers wishing to extend this hike another half-mile can follow this northward trail to its intersection with the A.T., where they can turn right and return to the parking area. Otherwise, to remain on this loop, follow the Ramble Trail to its junction with the Chambersburg Water Line, a hiking path, and turn right to follow the line on a direct route back to the picnic and parking area.

Other Activities: Visitors interested in exploring the rich history of iron production will find interpretive exhibits and information at the blacksmith shop and the iron-furnace monument. Energetic hikers may choose to take a longer hike to explore the charcoal hearths on the Charcoal Hearth and Thaddeus Stevens Trail Loop. That hike begins at the iron-furnace monument. The swimming pool and playground offer respite for younger hikers, and the

Caledonia State Park. (Photo by Leanna Joyner)

Totem Pole Playhouse offers entertainment in the summer months. Visitors may choose to take a short drive 10 miles west to Chambersburg to visit one farmhouse of abolitionist John Brown at 225 King Street. From this house, John Brown laid the semifinal plans for his raid on Harpers Ferry. Thirteen miles east of Caledonia is the town of Gettysburg, the drive to which on U.S. 30 echoes the path that General Jubal A. Early and his Rebels took on their way to the famous battle.

Pine Grove Furnace

The ironmaster's mansion is considered by many to have been part of the network of Underground Railroad stations. A hidden room is accessed through a small door in the floor of a closet beneath the main staircase. A short, four-rung ladder descends to a squat room roughly 8 feet by 6 feet that connects to similar rooms on two sides through passageways built into the rock walls of the foundation. The secret space is mentioned in the Appalachian Long Distance Hikers Association's *Appalachian Trail Thru-Hikers' Companion* as an Underground Railroad stop, although the legitimacy of the site is unverified.

The furnace was established in 1764. A long lineage of ironmasters owned the iron works at Pine Grove, including Michael Ege of Boiling Springs Iron Works and later his son Peter. Under Peter Ege's ownership, the mansion was built in 1827. Local legend suggests that the architectural design, predating what would become known as "I houses" and insisted upon by his wife, Jane, was particular to Underground Railroad stops, pointing to the circular windows in the attic, facing south and east, as a "message" to freedom-seekers of safe haven ahead.

No firsthand accounts verifiably attest to there being an Underground Railroad stop at the Pine Grove mansion, but the possibility certainly exists, and other experts have identified it as one possible stop within the vast network of sites.

Pine Grove Furnace Hike

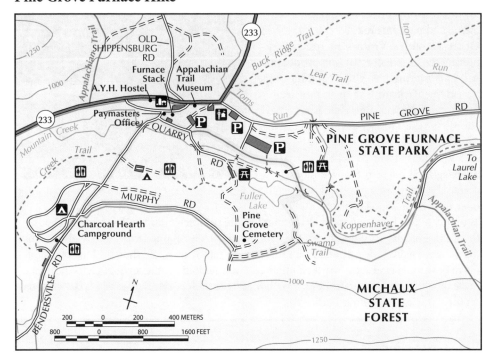

Distance: 1 mile

Trailhead parking: If arriving from Caledonia State Park, travel north on Pa. 233. From I-81, take Exit 37 for Pa. 233. Follow 233 south for 8 miles. At the stop sign, indicating the junction for Pa. 233 and State Road 2008, the visitor-information center and ranger station will be directly ahead of you in a white building. The information center hosts displays and information about the history of the furnace. Turning right from the stop sign, pass a drive on your left for park vehicles only, and reach a second drive on your left marked with signs for the campground. There is a day-use parking area beside the store to your right, and the Appalachian Trail Museum is situated in the former grist mill just across the street.

Description: From the parking area beside the store, turn right, then turn left at the paymaster's cabin to follow Quarry Road a short distance, past the old furnace stack. Just beyond a turn for another parking area, pick up the Appalachian Trail (indicated by white-paint blazes) below the museum to the left. The path follows an easy course around Fuller Lake, which once served as the quarry for the iron ore smelted at this furnace. Hikers often enjoy a cool dip in the lake during the hottest of summer months.

On the east side of the lake, turn right to stay along the lake shore a short distance

Ironmasters Mansion at Pine Grove Furnace may have served as a stop along the Underground Railroad for escaped slaves. (Photo by Leanna Joyner)

farther to reach Murphy Road. Pass Pine Grove Cemetery on your right, and continue on Murphy Road until it intersects the campground access road. Turn right to return to the parking area. Before returning to your vehicle, visit the hiker hostel, formerly the ironmaster's mansion (see above).

Other Activities: Throughout the summer, the Appalachian Trail Museum is definitely worth a visit. Railroad Bed Road offers a pleasant, if brief, opportunity to bicycle two miles to Laurel Lake from the furnace stack. In the summer, opportunities to swim at Laurel and Fuller lakes offer relief from the heat. Not far from Pine Grove Furnace is the town of Mount Holly Springs, another stop on the Underground Railroad, and a town through which the Confederate Army passed on its way to Gettysburg. The short hike offered at Pine Grove Furnace is a great half-day hike to couple with the short hike at Boiling Springs (see page 14).

Mount Holly Springs

Roughly three miles west of the Appalachian Trail crossing of Pa. 34 is Mount Holly Springs, another ironworks town, settled in 1750 and situated on the banks of the Yellow Breeches Creek, similar to the A.T. town of Boiling Springs. Mount Holly Springs also served as a destination for freedom-seekers.[14] Those who did not stop here often continued on to Boiling Springs, about five miles on a direct route or 11.3 miles by way of the Appalachian Trail today.

Fugitives hosted by one of six "conductors" in Gettysburg often advanced to York Springs and then either Mount Holly Springs, Wrightsville, or directly to Harrisburg.[15]

Boiling Springs, Pennsylvania

The northbound Appalachian Trail enters the town of Boiling Springs from the southeast, skirts the edge of Children's Lake, and passes near the bubbling springs that give the town its name. The town's planner, Daniel Kaufman, who laid out the streets of this community, was also a host for fugitive slaves on the Underground Railroad. Fleeing slaves took refuge in his barn. Kaufman's home was located at 301 Front Street, just across the middle of the lake from the Appalachian Trail. A historical marker at that location commemorates Kaufman's contributions to the town and the Underground Railroad. The sign mentions a highly publicized case in which Kaufman was tried for providing food and transportation to runaways. It was the second of two cases against Kaufman for the same reason. The first was reversed on appeal in the Pennsylvania Supreme Court.

Kaufman hid slaves in his barn as well in the dense thickets of Island Grove, a short distance downstream on Yellow Breeches Creek from the town of Boiling Springs. The obituary for Kaufman that ran in *The Evening Sentinel* on July 26, 1902, described it as a place only the initiated could navigate. Slaves in groups

This was the home of Daniel Kaufman who was tried and found guilty of assisting runaway slaves by providing them shelter at his barn in Island Grove. (Photo by Leanna Joyner)

The Ege family, who operated the iron furnace in Boiling Springs, lived in this mansion from 1847 to 1859. During some of that time family members may have assisted escaped slaves on the Underground Railroad. (Photo by Leanna Joyner)

as great as ten or twelve were piloted there to rest and be fed before moving on again.[16]

Other residents of Boiling Springs aided slaves. Stephen Weakley allowed his barn to be used to shelter a group of thirteen slaves that had previously been at Kaufman's barn. They were later transported by a wagon driven by Thomas Weakley.[17]

A white mansion that sits on a hill just above the lakeshore at 108 Bucher Hill was purportedly a stop on the Underground Railroad. Author Richard Tritt, in his *A Place Called Boiling Springs*, tentatively states that it might have been a stop during Peter and Jane Ege's residence there from 1847 to 1859. According to Tritt, the legend includes tunnels leading to the paymaster's house, the stone house on the opposite lakeshore from the mansion, as well as a "compartment on the third floor" meant to conceal slaves.[18] (The Bucher family in the late 1980s sold the lake, shoreline, and other property to the Appalachian Trail Conservancy and the National Park Service for the permanent protection of the Trail.)

Others theorize about secret passages and rooms in the hill across the road from the old ironmaster's mansion here.[19] The mansion is privately owned and not open to the public. Visitors to Boiling Springs will have to draw their own conclusions about whether the hills surrounding the mansion host secret caves, whether an underground tunnel connects the mansion to the stone paymaster's structure across the lake, and whether this ironmaster's mansion ever welcomed self-liberated slaves.

Boiling Springs Children's Lake Loop

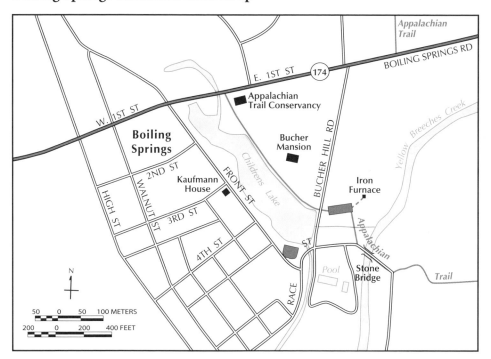

Distance: 0.7 mile

Description: In Boiling Springs, start your walk at the Appalachian Trail Conservancy office at 4 East First Street. Hike trail-south along the lakeshore. As you approach the remains of the iron furnace, take note of the large mansion on your left. It was the former home of ironmaster Michael Ege and later his son, Peter. It now bears the name the Bucher Mansion for its subsequent purchase by the Bucher family.

Instead of turning right along the outflow of the lake, continue across the street on the Appalachian Trail through the gravel parking area to the old iron furnace. Cross the footbridge at the corner of the parking area. Follow the white blazes on the trees, and reach Race Street. As you weave through the trees along Yellow Breeches Creek, gaze upstream to imagine the dense thickets of Island Grove that concealed groups of escaped slaves.

At Race Street, the A.T. continues left over the bridge and then over the railroad tracks before turning left off the road. For this hike and tour of Boiling Springs history, turn right. Pass the community pool on your left, and rejoin the lakeshore on your clockwise traverse.

The first stone structure you reach on your right along the lakeshore was formerly the paymaster's house. It is rumored to have tunnels leading beneath it to the big white mansion on the opposite shore. This is part of several legends suggesting the mansion was an Underground Railroad stop.

Continue on Front Street. Reach Daniel Kaufmann's house and historical marker at 305 Front Street on your left. Continue to First Street, and make a right to conclude your hike at the ATC office.

Next Stops

From Caledonia, Pine Grove Furnace, Boiling Springs, or Mount Holly Springs, escaped slaves were generally headed to either Harrisburg or Carlisle on the ever-changing web of secrecy that lead them to other northern states or to Canada.

Also in Pennsylvania

Routes led from Philadelphia through Quakertown and Bethlehem,[20] and, from Bethlehem, the route could have led to one of two places where it would intersect with the current route of the Appalachian Trail:

Palmerton

Fugitives likely followed the shores of the Lehigh River from Bethlehem northward until reaching Palmerton.[21]

East Stroudsburg

Located just a few miles from Delaware Water Gap, through which the Appalachian Trail passes, East Stroudsburg was the home of Robert Brown, son of John Brown, whose notorious raid on Harpers Ferry in 1859 was a precursor to the Civil War.[22] From Brown's home, fugitives could have continued the few miles to reach the Delaware River and follow it upstream and north. Hikers today cross over the Delaware River on an interstate-highway bridge into or from New Jersey.

More information about the trail in those areas, along with more history of nearby points, can be found in the *Appalachian Trail Guide to Maryland–Northern Virginia* and the *Appalachian Trail Guide to Pennsylvania,* available at the Ultimate Appalachian Trail Store* (*www.atctrailstore.org*).

Harpers Ferry

Harpers Ferry, addressed on its own as a war zone later in this book, is also an intersection of old Underground Railroad routes and the current A.T. Slaves, disguised to preserve their identity, were passengers on trains bound for Pittsburgh with tickets purchased from Harpers Ferry, for example.[32]

The Chesapeake and Ohio Canal towpath, in Maryland along the northern shore of the Potomac River, offered a path to runaways from the Washington, D.C., vicinity.[33] In this instance, the A.T. may actually overlap the path of runaway slaves for two miles between Harpers Ferry and a gap in the Blue Ridge downstream. Underground Railroad scholar Wilber H. Siebert called canals "convenient highways to liberty for a number of self-reliant fugitives and were considered safer than public roads."[34]

New York

Arriving by land or water, slaves who reached New York City would take a course along the Hudson River north to Albany and Troy before heading west toward Niagara Falls and Canada. The Appalachian Trail now crosses the wide Hudson River over the Bear Mountain Bridge, just northeast of Bear Mountain–Harriman State Park and east of the town of Ft. Montgomery.[35]

Massachusetts

According to an Upper Housatonic Valley African-American Heritage Trail brochure, Gulf Road between Dalton and Lanesborough has a cave beneath it that may have been used as a path along the Underground Railroad for passengers coming from Lebanon Mountain. Nearby Wizard's Glen was a small community of blacks in the early 1820s.[36] The Appalachian Trail is colocated with Gulf Road briefly.

Vermont

The West Vermont "railroad" route that ran parallel to the western boundary of the state included the present A.T. trail towns of Manchester Center and Bennington. Following what is now U.S. 7, the West Vermont route extended to Middlebury and eventually on to St. Albans and on into Canada.[37] The Appalachian Trail roughly parallels U.S. 7 to the east, offset by as few as five miles or as many as 20 miles before turning east toward New Hampshire, just beyond the U.S. 4 crossing east of Rutland at Killington.

New Hampshire and Maine

The Underground Railroad station at Canaan, located to the east of the A.T. at its crossing of Grafton Turnpike, likely would have used this road as a corridor northwest to Lyme and then on to the Connecticut River, where freedom-seekers could follow it north, on a route similar to modern-day I-91.[38]

According to Underground Railroad researcher Wilber Siebert:

> "James Furber, who lived in Canaan for several years, is said to have made trips to Lyme about once a fortnight with refugees received by him."[39]

and

> "The Grand Trunk, extending from Portland, Maine, through the northern parts of New Hampshire and Vermont into Canada, occasionally gave passes to fugitives and would always take reduced fares for his class of passengers."[40]

In this instance, the Grand Trunk railroad intersected the current A.T. at one of two locations—either at Maine 26 in Maine near Speck Mountain or in New Hampshire on U.S. 2 just east of Gorham.

Private D.W.C. Arnold of the 22nd New York State Militia. The photo was taken in 1862 on Camp Hill, just a few steps away from the present-day headquarters of the Appalachian Trail Conservancy in Harpers Ferry, West Virginia. (Library of Congress)

The Civil War

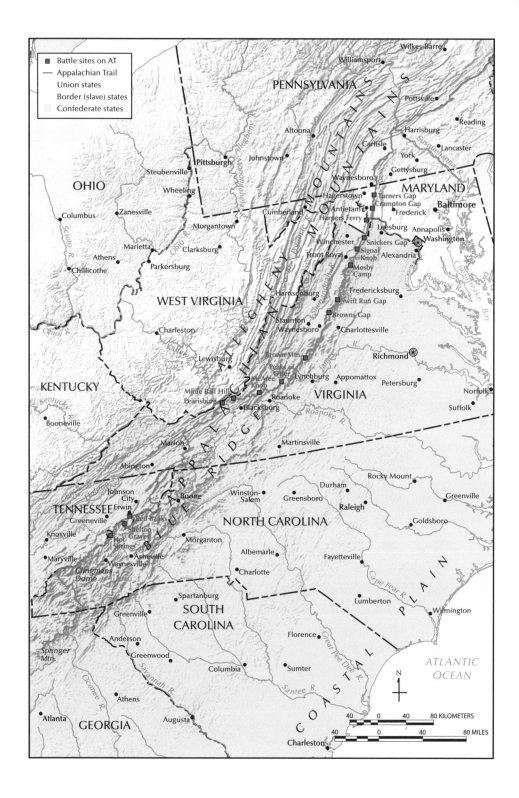

Mountain Battles in Southern Appalachia

Many sources simplify the Unionism of the western North Carolina mountain inhabitants by pointing to the fact that large landowners and townspeople of the South tended to be Confederates and that people who lived in the mountains of the Appalachians generally owned smaller farms and did not have slaves.[41] Scholars and authors of *The Heart of Confederate Appalachia: Western North Carolina in the Civil War* explore this premise and reveal deeper complexities of political affiliation and alliances preceding and during the war.

Unionists of Appalachia were not synonymous with the antislavery movement.[42] While only about ten percent of households in western North Carolina counties owned slaves,[43] the alliance with the Federalist cause was driven by patriotism for the United States and in opposition to the members of the wealthy and ruling upper class who controlled their state and took it upon themselves to revolt.[44] Bound by communities rather than socioeconomic ties, people of the mountains were varied in education, skin color, and class. They may have been tenant farmers, freed slaves, Cherokee, small farmers working their own property, or small-scale farmers with a few slaves, but their cause was not abolition. While many opposed the division of the Union, others supported the Confederate cause.

The groundswell for Confederate sympathies was greatest at the outset of the war, even in western North Carolina. In fact, while five counties that touch the A.T. in western North Carolina opposed secession in February 1861, three other counties the A.T. passes through supported the movement.[45]

North Carolina's neighbor to the west was decidedly more Federalist from the outset. The eastern third of Tennessee, 29 counties in total, voted against secession in a February 9, 1861, vote.[46] This Union enclave in the South was a constant source of worry for North Carolina Confederates throughout the war and later served as recruiting grounds for North Carolinians aligned with the Union.

That division of loyalties split communities and families. In the far western counties of North Carolina that today touch the Appalachian Trail, recruiters solicited for both sides.

Participation in the Confederate forces by western North Carolinians included:

- 25th North Carolina Regiment, led by Brigadier General Thomas Clingman, with troops hailing from eight western North Carolina counties and organized in August 1861.
- 69th North Carolina Regiment, also called Thomas' Legion, made up of three companies of native Americans from Quallatown and led by Colonel William Holland Thomas and organized in September 1862.
- 64th North Carolina Regiment, organized in the summer of 1862 with recruits largely from Madison County.

Participation in Union forces made up of western North Carolinians included the 2nd and 3rd North Carolina Mounted Infantry, organized in October 1863 and June 1864, respectively, with recruits from eastern Tennessee and western North Carolina, including Madison County. Those brigades were eventually led by George W. Kirk.

Following the Confederate Conscription Act of April 1862 that required military service by able men of certain ages, Rebel forces were flush. However, those forced into service commonly deserted and returned home or felt even more compelled to join the Union forces.[47] The North Carolina 64th was "particularly plagued by desertions," according to authors of *The Heart of Confederate Appalachia,* who explain that, "at one point, 300 men abandoned the regiment together, most of whom who returned to Madison County to hide."[48] This tension, along with other events, led to the bloody "Shelton Laurel massacre" (see page 26) and battles and skirmishes in southern Appalachia between brothers and cousins in Hot Springs, North Carolina, and in Chestoa, Tennessee.

The Appalachian Trail today passes nearby sites of skirmishes, the stories of which are seldom told. Civil War history in southern Appalachia is scattered across these ridges and river valleys where the Appalachian Trail now passes and included the players of the 64th Regiment, Confederate States of America (CSA), and the 2nd and 3rd North Carolina Mounted Infantry, United States of America (USA).

Hot Springs, North Carolina

The Appalachian Trail passes through the small town of Hot Springs, North Carolina. Called Warm Springs until the 1890s, the long-time resort town is situated along the shore of the French Broad River, just inside the border with Tennessee. Large river valleys, like the French Broad, offered favorable routes for military movement through the mountains during the Civil War. They offered a means for Unionists of East Tennessee to invade North Carolina territory; those invasions sparked fights, destroyed property, and recruited for the Union cause. As a result of its location, Hot Springs was frequented by troops from both sides. In October 1863, George W. Kirk and between 600 and 800 men of the North Carolina

View of Hot Springs, North Carolina. (Photo by Leanna Joyner)

Mounted Infantry[49] raided, then held, the town. Skirmishes occurred there on October 20, 23, and 26. Another clash took place on November 26, 1863.[50]

The instability in the mountains of western North Carolina prompted armory personnel in Asheville to consider its relocation to a site further south. The attack on Warm Springs illustrated the precarious security of Confederate supplies, so, following this Union incursion into Confederate territory, the decision was finally solidified to relocate the armory.[51]

While the protracted Union control of Warm Springs in October 1863 was the most significant military action of the Civil War in this location, the town saw its fair share of traveling brigades. In April 1865, near the end of the war and just after the launch of Union General George Stoneman's raid through southwest Virginia and North Carolina, Ohio infantry were ordered from Greenville, Tennessee, southward through the French Broad River Valley to Asheville. The Ohioans passed through this pretty town, nestled deep among the mountains, just before engaging in the Battle of Asheville.[52]

Lovers Leap—Silvermine Trail Loop Hike

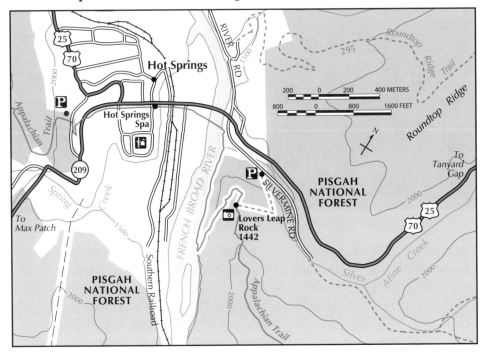

Distance: 1.6 miles

Difficulty: Easy

Trailhead directions: Arrive in Hot Springs on U.S. 25/70. If arriving from the east, you will crest the mountain range at Tanyard Gap, passing beneath an overpass for the A.T., and continue three miles to reach River Road on your right. Turn right on River Road before crossing the river or arriving in town. If arriving from the west, after passing through town and crossing over the French Broad River bridge, make your first left, onto River Road. About 0.1 mile on River Road, take a sharp left turn on Silvermine Road, between a residence on the left and open space on your right, to pass under U.S. 25/70. Continue on this road, past a sign indicating the A.T., to reach the USDA Forest Service Silvermine Trailhead.

Description: From the trailhead parking lot, begin walking back toward the river on the road you just entered to join the Appalachian Trail, marked by a sign on your left over a wooden bridge. Follow the path that parallels the French Broad River and shortly veer left up an incline, followed by several relatively steep switchbacks. Soon, reach a subtle junction with the Lovers Leap Overlook, evident by a few wooden steps and an open clearing on rocks that offers a panoramic view of the town of Hot Springs.

From the high point of this easy loop hike, one can gain expansive views of the surrounding mountains and the wide French Broad River Valley, which served as a frequent thoroughfare for Union troop movements in western North Carolina. It also offers a modern look at the Hot Springs Spa, where the 350-room Warm Springs Hotel was once located and served as George W. Kirk's headquarters for the month of October 1863, when it was under Union occupation.

The trail continues left from the junction with the overlook and shortly splits into two trails. The Appalachian Trail northbound continues on the right side of the fork, and the Silvermine Trail on the left returns to the parking area. Follow the left fork to continue on the Silvermine Trail and descend through a thick grove of rhododendron and moss-covered earth to a junction with a trail leading to a group-camping area. Remain on the Silvermine Trail by taking the switchback left at this junction, to descend farther and parallel a creek bed on your right before reaching the trailhead parking area.

Other Activities: Near Hot Springs, hikers can drive up to another favored Appalachian Trail vista at Max Patch. From the Max Patch trailhead, visitors can follow a ¼-mile side trail to the top of the open area for views southwest to the Great Smoky Mountains and east to the Black Mountain range. Picnics, kite-flying, and sunsets are among the favored accompaniments to this short hike. Outdoor adventure guides in Hot Springs offer whitewater rafting on the French Broad River. Visits to the town of Hot Springs rarely feel complete without following up outdoor activities with a soak in a private tub at the Hot Springs Spa.

The Shelton Laurel Massacre and the Mysteries of the Shelton Graves

While other areas of western North Carolina may have wavered between supporting the Confederacy and supporting the Union, Shelton Laurel was a Unionist enclave from the outset, its roots dating back to its settlers' participation in the Revolutionary War.[53]

Those leanings of the residents of Shelton Laurel brought them to the attention of Confederates, who first applied pressure for recruitment and later punished the community for its Confederate desertions and allegiance to the Union cause.

The incident now known locally as the Shelton Laurel Massacre or Atrocity began in late 1862 with the withholding of precious salt, necessary for the preservation of meat for the winter, from the residents of Shelton Laurel in an effort to "persuade" them to participate in the Secessionist cause. Under this pressure, as many as fifty people from Shelton Laurel, including some Confederate deserters and a few known Union raiders, traveled to the county seat of Marshall in January 1863 to claim the salt owed them. They also took merchandise from other stores in the town and harassed the family, including two bedridden children, of one prominent Confederate, Colonel Lawrence Allen, commander of the 64th North Carolina Regiment.[54]

In retaliation for the "salt raid" on Marshall, the 64th North Carolina Regiment under the leadership of Allen and Lt. Colonel James A. Keith swept into Shelton Laurel, home to 137 Sheltons, to squash the pro-Union activity. With news of the Confederates approaching, many men scattered. Women were tortured—including an 85-year-old who was whipped and hung—in a vain effort to extract information about participants in the raid. The Rebel retribution for the salt raid captured fifteen male hostages, mainly those too old or too young to have participated in the raid. Thirteen were executed and their bodies dumped in a shallow snow grave a few miles from Shelton Laurel.[55] Aghast at the brutality of the massacre, North Carolina Governor Zebulon B. Vance ordered an inquiry and pushed for the removal of Keith from service. Keith, 35 and one of Madison County's wealthiest men, was court-martialed and retired from official duty after two years as a fugitive.[56] (Vance earlier had succeeded Thomas Clingman, namesake of Clingmans Dome, in the U.S. House.)

By October of that year, the 2nd North Carolina Mounted Infantry (a Union force) was formed in Tennessee, with recruits hailing from Madison, Jackson, and Cherokee counties in North Carolina. Among the enlisted were eight Sheltons and six Hensleys,[57] presumably from Shelton Laurel and elsewhere in Madison County

View of Shelton Laurel from Firescald Knob. (Photo by Leanna Joyner)

along the border with Tennessee. The 2nd North Carolina Mounted Infantry performed duties at Cumberland Gap, Tennessee, in late 1863. On December 19, 1863, David Shelton, left the unit and returned home without leave.[58]

Shelton, who had enlisted in Company E of the 2nd Mounted Infantry, remained at home or in the neighborhood until June 1864, when he joined Colonel George W. Kirk, who was recruiting in the area for his newly formed 3rd North Carolina Mounted Infantry. Shelton returned to service and took part in a raid on Camp Vance on June 28. After participating in the raid, Shelton again returned home without leave, supposedly to allow an injured foot to heal.[59]

On July 19, 1864, while near his Shelton Laurel home, he and others were on Butt Mountain near Cold Spring. A couple Rebels arrived and killed David and four others. The Appalachian Trail passes by the gravestones for David Shelton, William Shelton, and Milliard Haire, buried in a common grave. The other two purportedly are buried together in an unmarked grave a few hundred yards north.[60]

The family lore surrounding the murders on Big Butt Mountain insists that David and his nephew William were home recruiting for the Union cause. Accordingly, their recruitment efforts won them the scrutiny of Confederates. In the mountain-top cabin, David and William with 12 others—including two other enlisted men and their fathers and Milliard Haire, a 13-year old scout who had been sent a day earlier to warn the men of Rebels in the area—were ambushed. Five were killed, another five were taken prisoner, and the rest escaped.

That story is the one commonly recounted in other books about the Appalachian Trail—in the ALDHA *Appalachian Trail Thru-Hikers' Companion* as well as in J.R. Tate's *Walkin' with the Ghost Whisperers*. The *Companion* identifies the killers as Confederate sympathizers. Tate's research relies heavily on the family's account of history and points to the 64th North Carolina's Keith, who had a poor reputation in the community following the Shelton Massacre. It's difficult to know the certainty of his role in the ambush on the mountain or if he was an easy scapegoat for the continued hardships of the Shelton family.

Among the men in the cabin, six already had enlisted in Company E of the 2nd Mounted Infantry, including David and William. At least one other, W.S. Ray, had enlisted in the 3rd North Carolina Mounted. [61] According to Tate, Hampton Burgess, Jr., had enlisted.[62] Six members of the party at the cabin had not enlisted: Two of them were fathers and likely considered too old to fight, and one was the 13-year old Milliard. That leaves the possibility that the remaining three, Alan Lisenbee and two others unnamed in Tate's account, may have been potential recruits, as the family asserts.

In the early-morning attack, Milliard was shot first, followed by David and William. The other two deaths are recounted in this way by Tate:

> *Hampton Burgess and Isaac Shelton, both civilians who had come up to the cabin the day before to spend the night with their two soldier sons, managed to make it through the cabin window. They high-tailed it up the trail but were soon overtaken by Keith's men and killed…. The two fathers were buried in another unmarked grave a couple of hundred yards farther north.*[63]

A distinctly different story is told of this incident in the investigative records of pension claims filed by Elizabeth Shelton following the death of her husband, David. Special Agent G.H. Ragsdale of the Pensions Claim Office investigated the claim. It is likely that all six men in Company E who were present on the mountain on July 19 left the command at the same time, against orders from Colonel Kirk. The investigation showed that men in the regiment had asked for the opportunity to stop at home and that Kirk, being overburdened with prisoners and captured supplies following the raid on Camp Vance, could spare no one. He also pointed out to the men the dangers of stopping behind the Confederate lines. The testimony of J. M. Sprinkles, who was also under Kirk's command at the time, said that, "passing by Laurel, a number of the men who lived there dropped out, against said Kirk's orders, and Kirk swore he would have them shot and made a great fuss about men leaving him at such a time."[64]

That poses another, although unlikely, possibility: that Kirk made good on his threat to punish and make an example of the desertions from his command. It's

The graves of Daniel Shelton, William Shelton, and Millard Haire along the Appalachian Trail in North Carolina. (Photo by Leanna Joyner)

difficult to know whether Kirk would have sent any of his men, during a time of limited resources and within enemy territory, to dispose of deserters, but it is among the possibilities to be considered.

The damning summary of the investigation by Special Agent Ragsdale also says: "This man [David] enlisted in said company and remained with it long enough to draw $31.83 worth of clothing and then deserted." It added: "This man and a number of others of the same class fell out of line and refused to go any further. They found other associates with whom they had been laying out. They made their hiding place on Butt Mountain and supposed the rebels could not find them and could not get up the mountain even if this hiding place was known. From this location they made raids, and…pressed whatever property they could find. The rebels regarded them as a band of robbers and were anxious to find them. They finally succeeded in slipping up on the party and almost annihilated it. Five men were killed, and a number were wounded." His report concludes with the emphasis that "they were not with any command when shot but with other men who were known as common robbers."

The family story recounts them as Union heroes home recruiting for the cause and murdered for their loyalty. The federal investigation cites the motivation of the murderers to prevent further theft in the community by robbers held up in their mountain hideaway.

No substantial evidence is available to suggest that Keith was involved in the murders on the mountain nor is it reasonable to assume that Kirk could have orchestrated an attack, considering he was overburdened with captured prisoners and supplies and expected an attack at any time from Rebels following his unit.

Were they heroes or criminals? Deserters or recruiters? Why were they on the ridgecrest rather than with their wives and children? More than 150 years have passed, and only the mountain knows the truth.

The gravestones for David and William were procured from the federal government in 1915 by two preachers, the Reverends Frederick Webb and Monroe Shelton, and hauled up by an ox sled. Since Milliard wasn't in the service, his place in the common grave was unmarked until 1996, when his relatives installed a marker in his memory. Unfortunately, the date on Milliard's marker indicates his death as July 1, 1863, rather than July 19, 1864, adding to the confusion about this site's history. A question also remains why relatives chose to overlook marking the common grave of the other two men killed in the same incident.

Shelton Graves Hike

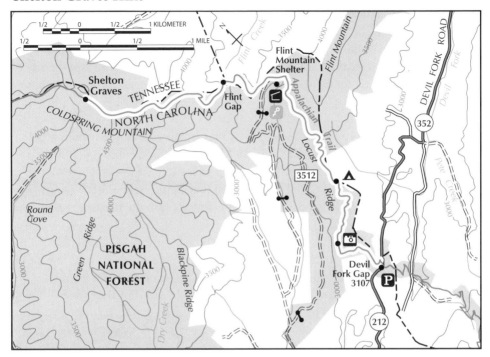

Distance: 11.4 miles round trip
Difficulty: Moderate
Trailhead directions: From I-26, take Exit 5 for Flag Pond. All traffic is directed east to a T-junction. Take a left on Higgins Creek Road to a stop sign at the intersection with Tenn. 81/ U.S. 23. Make a right, and pass through the small town of Flag Pond. Look for Devil Fork Road (Tenn. 352) on your left, and take it to the height of the land, which serves as the boundary for North Carolina and Tennessee. Ample parking is available on the left side of the road. A few steps down the road into North Carolina (east), you will easily identify the Trail heading *north* over a stile and through a field. You want to pick up the A.T. heading *south*, found just across the street and a few steps up the embankment.
Description: The hike from Devil Fork Gap begins moderately with an ascent to reach Flint Gap Shelter in 2.5 miles. Just beyond the shelter, you will reach a fork in the Trail; take the path on the right, watching carefully for trail markers. Farther, the trail descends to Flint Gap in another 0.8 mile before beginning a gradual approach to the ridge of Cold Spring Mountain. This new trail parallels the previous route, so visitors need to take a side trail of approximately 30 feet to reach the graves.

December 29, 1864: The Battle of Red Banks

The Appalachian Trail crosses over the Nolichucky River at Chestoa, three miles from Erwin, Tennessee, in Unicoi County. During the Civil War, Unicoi County was still part of Washington County, and the area now known as Chestoa was called Greasy Cove and extended through what is now Erwin. On the Appalachian Trail bridge over the Nolichucky, hikers pass less than a mile from the site of a bloody battle between neighbors that raged in this narrow slot of the Nolichucky River.

It was in predawn darkness in the deep of winter in December 1864 when 400 Union troops from the 3rd North Carolina Mounted Infantry under Colonel George W. Kirk (see above) discovered a camp of resting Confederates from the 64th North Carolina. Often called the Battle of Red Banks or the Battle of Greasy Cove, it was a victory for the Federals, who benefited from the hardships already faced by Rebel troops.

The Confederates were suffering from the cold. Many had no shoes, and few had tents. Those without shoes suffered additional injury—bloodied feet from the hard snow and ice. Their forces were as large as the Union's, but they were ill-equipped and too surprised to effectively fight back. The attack killed 73 Rebels and sent the rest of them running. They retreated south, pursued by the Union troops toward the North Carolina border at Sams Gap at the North Carolina and Tennessee border, where the A.T. today crosses as well.[65]

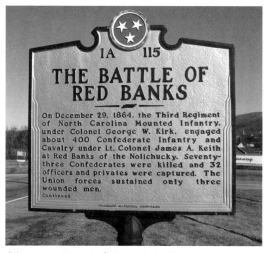

(Tennessee Historical Commission)

The leadership of the 64th is a bit in question. Technically, they would not have been led by Lt. Colonel James A. Keith, since he had earlier been court-martialed and retired from his post because of the incidents at Shelton Laurel. However, first-hand accounts from a man in the 64th report that Keith was there and leading the action. Historian Christina Tipton speculates he was fighting without a formal commission.[66]

Cliff Ridge Hike

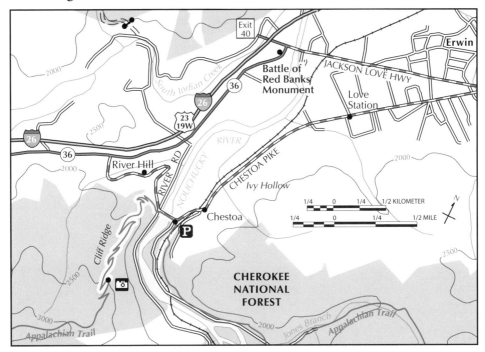

Distance: 3 miles round trip

Difficulty: Moderate

Trailhead directions: Take Exit 40 off I-26. Heading toward Erwin on Jackson-Love Highway (Tenn. 36), you will pass a historical marker for the Battle of Red Banks just before making a right turn onto Chestoa Pike, which parallels the interstate. On Chestoa Pike, you then will pass the Mountain Inn & Suites, the site of the Battle of Red Banks, and a convenience store. Turn left onto River Road, also marked by a brown sign that denotes whitewater rafting, and travel for 0.4 mile to a four-way stop at the Chestoa Bridge, which the A. T. crosses. For the largest parking area, cross the bridge, and turn right immediately onto Jones Branch Road, where roadside parking is available on the right a few yards from the intersection.

Description: Beginning at the trailhead, cross the bridge on foot. Gaze downstream toward the bend in the river to the site of the Battle of Red Banks, just less than a mile away. On the far side of the bridge from the trailhead parking area, face upstream, and walk a few paces to find the double white blazes indicating the Trail's ascent of the hill on steps. The first 1.5 miles of this hike is a steady climb to reach the views afforded from Cliff Ridge. From the ridge, you gain a plentiful view of the Nolichucky River and the railroad tracks. Often you can hear the trains' whistles echoing off the deep canyon walls of this narrow river valley. Complete the hike by returning north on the Trail to your vehicle.

Other Activities: Unicoi County offers the chance for lovers of nature to relax in campgrounds or hike more than 63 miles of trails in the 640,000 acres of Cherokee National

Forest. While in Unicoi County, visitors may enjoy exploring the recently protected 10,000-acre tract of wilderness called Rocky Fork for fishing, hiking, or mountain biking. Another relatively short and rewarding hike on the Appalachian Trail to Beauty Spot begins with a short drive from Erwin. Visitors who drive east on Tenn. 395/Rock Creek Road to an A.T. Trailhead at Indian Grave Gap can proceed trail-north 2.5 miles to Beauty Spot for a picnic and views.

More information about the trail in this area, along with more history of nearby points, can be found in the *Appalachian Trail Guide to Tennessee–North Carolina*, available at the Ultimate Appalachian Trail Store* (*www.atctrailstore.org*).

Union Occupation of Pearisburg, Virginia

Over the winter of 1861–62, a Union strategy was developed in Washington to invade southwest Virginia to seize lead and salt mines and destroy the Virginia and Tennessee Railroad that was vital to the Confederacy's supply lines to Richmond, its capital.

On May 6, 1862, a Union scouting mission was sent to investigate The Narrows of the New River for remaining Confederate supplies. The scouts, originating from Princeton in soon-to-be-West Virginia, found the area unguarded and without any materials so they pushed on east to the Giles County Courthouse in what today is known as Pearisburg, Virginia. The first to arrive in Pearisburg were companies H, I, and K of the 23rd Ohio, led by Major James M. Comly and accompanied by Captain George W. Gilmore's cavalry. They sent word back to Lt. Colonel Rutherford B. Hayes, their commander, of the capture of prisoners and large stores of supplies, including "two hundred and fifty barrels of flour and everything else."[67]

On May 7, Hayes, 38, future president of the United States[68], arrived to act as a reinforcement to the party of invaders camped south of town at the base of Angel's Rest and to secure the advantageous capture of supplies. He was accompanied by William McKinley, 19, a newly promoted commissary sergeant and also a future president. (The 23rd Ohio, in addition to two future presidents, also was home then to men who would become six generals, a U.S. Supreme Court justice, a U.S. senator, four U.S. representatives, four governors, and four lieutenant governors.) Among the spoils now in their custody was corn, corn meal, sugar, salt, ammunition, and tools, with a worth totaling more than $5,000. Holding on to the supplies would prove to be a challenge for the Union, because of its limited forces to both guard against invasion and keep watch over the bounty.

Hayes and his roughly 600 men held Pearisburg from May 6 to the predawn hours of May 10. The reinforcements Hayes had repeatedly requested never arrived, and an early-morning attack by a Confederate army of 2,500 to 3,000 under General Henry Heth sent a wounded Hayes and his men in retreat to The Narrows and eventually back to Princeton. They left behind the goods they had seized and their prisoners.

> Hayes repeatedly hailed the New River in the area as "romantic" and Pearisburg as a "neat, pretty village with a most magnificent surrounding country both as regards scenery and cultivation."

The number of dead and wounded as a result of this battle was fairly small. Union casualties included three killed and several wounded, none seriously, and Confederates suffered two dead and four wounded.

According to Hayes' diary entry of May 8, Union Sergeant Edward A. Abbott and his scout on patrol said they spotted a Confederate officer with a large spy glass "examining the village from a very high mountain whose summit, two miles distant, overlooks the whole town."[69]

The Confederates' assessment of the limited number of the Union soldiers in Pearisburg is what helped shape their decision to invade. If this decision were based in large part on information gathered by the perspective offered at this high vantage point, then this locale is indeed pivotal to the truncated Union control of Pearisburg. It may be that the officer stood on Angel's Rest. Angel's Rest—an outcropping along today's A.T. that overlooks the town of Pearisburg, The Narrows, and the New River—would have offered the perfect perspective to see the Union position in town.

Angel's Rest Hike

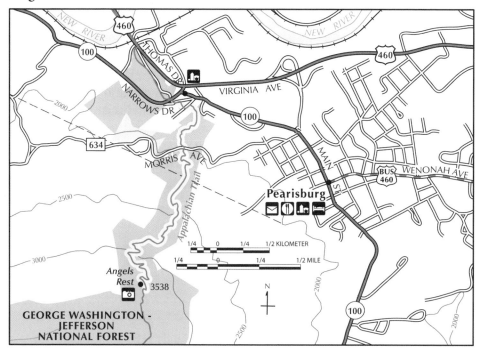

Distance: 6.2-miles

View of Pearisburg from Angel's Rest. (Photo by Leanna Joyner)

Difficulty: Strenuous

Trailhead directions: To access the trailhead at Va. 100, drive west on U.S. 460 from the town of Pearisburg toward the New River. Turn left on Va. 100/Narrows Road. The parking area is beyond a curve on the right, in 0.3 mile. A kiosk is located at the woodland edge near the parking area.

Description: From the kiosk, follow the side trail 0.2 mile to a four-way intersection. Turn right on the A.T. to hike south 2.9 miles to reach Angel's Rest. (Going straight at the four-way intersection takes you a short distance to Pearis Cemetery, the burial site for twelve Civil War veterans as well as the namesake of the town, Captain George Pearis, who fought in the Revolutionary War.) In a half-mile, cross paved Va. 634. The ascent becomes more challenging as you tackle the remaining 1,600 feet of elevation gain over the next two miles. As you gain the summit, a sign will indicate a short spur trail to the Angel's Rest overlook. The views and perspectives offered from this vista are worth the vigorous hike and afford an outlook that may have been the deciding factor in the Confederate retaking of Pearisburg in May 1862. A hike in the early months of spring offers budding trees and clear views below, while a visit in the fall offers a panorama of colors surrounding this section of the New River Valley. Upon reaching Angel's Rest and taking a rest of your own, return to your vehicle the way you arrived, this time heading north on an easy descent of the Appalachian Trail.

Other Activities: Take time to explore the historic areas of Pearisburg. The main intersection downtown is the area that would have been largely under Union control in May 1862—an area that includes the historic courthouse and the Andrew Johnston House occupied by the future presidents. Today, the house is run by the Giles County Historical Society as a museum and historical and genealogy research center.

More information about the trail in this area, along with more history of nearby points, can be found in the *Appalachian Trail Guide to Southwest Virginia,* available at the Ultimate Appalachian Trail Store* (*www.atctrailstore.org*).

CAMP AT MOUTH OF EAST RIVER, GILES COUNTY, VIRGINIA, May 11, 1862.

DEAREST: -- Since I wrote you last I have lived a great deal. Do you know that Giles Court-house was captured with a large amount of stores, etc., etc., by a party sent by me from Princeton? It was so bold and impudent! I went with six companies of the Twenty-third to reinforce. I soon found that unless further reinforced we were gone up. The enemy, three thousand strong, were within ten miles of us with a battery of artillery. We had none. The place, a lovely mountain village, was wholly indefensible except by a large force. I sent two couriers a day to beg for reinforcements for three days. None came. At the last moment the order came that I should retreat if attacked by a largely superior force. This was easy to say, but to do it safely, after waiting till the enemy is on you, is not a trifle. I was up every night. Had guards and pickets on every point of approach. Well, yesterday morning, I got up before daylight, and visited the outposts. Just at dawn, I heard the alarm guns. The enemy were coming even in greater force than we expected. Four regiments, a battery of guns, and a small force of cavalry. I had only nine

President Rutherford B. Hayes. (Library of Congress)

companies of the Twenty-third, much weakened by detachments guarding supply trains, etc., and two weak companies of cavalry. Not more than one-fourth of the enemy's strength. But all went on like clockwork. Baggage was loaded and started. Captains Drake and Sperry undertook to hold the enemy with their companies and Captain Gilmore's Cavalry until the rest could take position in rear of the town. I went out with Captains Drake and Sperry. Just before sunrise, May 10, a lovely morning, we saw the advancing battalions in line of battle in beautiful order. They were commanded, it is said, by General Heth. They opened first with cannon firing shell. The first personal gratification was to find that my horse stood it well. Soon I saw that the men were standing it well. As they came in range of our skirmishers, some fatal firing checked them; but they were rapidly closing around us. Now was the first critical moment: Could our men retreat without breaking into confusion or a rout? They retired slowly, stubbornly, in good spirits and in order! I got a scratch on the right knee, just drawing blood but spoiling my drawers. But what of that? Things were going well. The enemy now approached our main line. Could it retreat also in order, for I knew it must be forced back. Here was the crisis of our fate. They stood firmly. The enemy halted to get his guns in position again. Soon we were in a fair way to be surrounded. The men were ordered to retire slowly, firing as they went, to a ridge forty rods back, and then to form again. They did it to perfection, and I knew we were safe. From that time, for five hours, it was only exciting fun. The fight lasted seven hours, we retreating six and one-half miles until we came to a narrow pass where three of our companies could hold back any number. Here we were safe. The Twenty-third looked gloriously after this. We got off as by a miracle. We lost one killed, one wounded badly and a host slightly, in the regiment; about the same in the cavalry. Applause was never so sweet as when right in the midst of the struggle, Gilmore's Cavalry gave me three cheers for a sharp stroke by which I turned the column out of range of the enemy's guns, which, with infinite trouble, he had placed to sweep us. It was a retreat (which is almost a synonym for defeat) and yet we all felt grand over it. But warn't the men mad at somebody for leaving us? We were joined by a battery and the Thirtieth Regiment at 4 P. M. under Colonel Scammon, starting at the seasonable hour of 7 A. M.! We are now strong again, but driven from a most valuable position with a loss of stores we had captured worth thousands. I am reported dangerously wounded by some of the cowardly cavalry (not Gilmore's) who fled forty miles, reporting us "routed," "cut to pieces," and the like. Never was a man prouder of his regiment than I of the Twenty-third. I keep thinking how well they behaved.--Love to all. Affectionately, R. B. HAYES.

12th, A. M. -- Since writing the foregoing, we have got information which leads me to think it was probably well we were not reinforced. There would not have been enough to hold the position we had against so great a force as the enemy brought against us. You see we were twenty miles from their railroad, and only six to twelve hours from their great armies. . . .

[Hayes, Rutherford B., Diary and Letters, Volume II, Advance and Retreat 1862, pg. 266-268]

≈

Wind Rock and Minie Ball Hill

By 1864, Ulysses S. Grant had taken charge of the Union forces as the commanding general and established a multipronged approach to occupy all available military personnel of the Confederates. He hoped to stretch them so thin, between fighting battles and defending railroads and resources, that he could swiftly defeat them. By choking off supplies, he expected to weaken the Secessionist cause and destabilize life for citizens of the South as well as their military.

Included in early 1864 orders from Grant was the instruction to General George Crook to cut off the supply lines for the Confederates by severing the Virginia and Tennessee Railroad, a two-year-old strategy that had failed before at Pearisburg (see page 35). Crook was commander of the Kanawha Division of West Virginia forces.

Robert Whisonant, who has written about the geological significance of southwest Virginia in its role in the Civil War, describes the importance of the Virginia and Tennessee Railroad this way:

> *This vital railroad—Lincoln himself called it 'the gut of the Confederacy'—moved supplies and troops both east and west, but shipments to Richmond to feed the voracious Confederate war machine were especially crucial.*[70]

Crook crossed into Virginia from the new state of West Virginia on May 6 along the route of what is now I-77. This was Crook's first crossing during this raid of the future Appalachian Trail, where the Trail dips on its traverse of Brushy Mountain to pass over I-77. The more significant crossing of the A.T. route as part of this raid occurred on his return to West Virginia, following events on Cloyd's Mountain in Pualski County and at Central Depot (now Radford) to destroy the railroad bridge over the New River, which had been Rutherford Hayes' assignment back in 1862. (Hayes and McKinley, now a major, continued to serve under Crook.)

Crook's men arrived in Dublin, Virginia, and engaged Confederate fighters at Cloyd's Mountain on May 9. They gained a victory over a larger Confederate force despite its holding strong defensive positions.[71] After their defeat, the Confederates—led by John McCausland after Brigadier General Albert G. Jenkins was mortally wounded and captured—retreated to the New River crossing at Central Depot, anticipating a Union advance to destroy the rail line.

The next day, Union and Confederate forces clashed again, this time blasting one another across the river from a distance. Union forces again won and seized control of a 700-foot-long wooden bridge anchored on metal piers. They burned

View from Wind Rock. (Photo by Leanna Joyner)

the superstructure but failed to destroy the piers. Within five weeks, Confederate forces had rebuilt the bridge over the New River.[72]

With the mission apparently complete, Crook and his men began a trip back across the rugged Appalachians into West Virginia in the rain. They had their own supplies, as well as hostages and goods they had captured.

Crook did not choose the easiest route, along the New River, "perhaps fearing the potential for entrapment, particularly at the great gorge through The Narrows."[73] Instead, he chose a route over Salt Pond Mountain along the Salt Springs Turnpike.

On the way, they passed Mountain Lake, a natural, spring-fed lake that was known then, as it is now (with the A.T. along its boundaries), as a resort. The army, soaked by rain and pursued by Confederates, continued past the lake without stopping.

The journey along the turnpike was exceptionally difficult for them because of the heavy rains and steep, muddy roads. Mud pulled on the wheels of the wagon trains, the boots of the men, and the hooves of the horses. It was slippery. It had rained so much that spirits were soaked as well.

Future President Hayes kept a journal in which he recounted his experiences. Following the burning of the New River bridge on May 10, he reported "a fierce rainstorm" on May 11 and called the following day "a most disagreeable rainy day" as they traveled fifteen miles from Blacksburg to Salt Pond Mountain, for which the most memorable part was the mud and horrible roadway:

> *My brigade had charge of the [wagon] train. I acted as wagon-master; a long train to keep up. Rode all day in mud and rain back and forth…. Got to camp— no tents—at midnight. Mud; slept on wet ground without blankets. A horrible day, one of the worst of all my experience.*[74]

According to the *Appalachian Trail Guide to Central Virginia*, musket balls and other supplies were discarded under orders from Crook because of the sinking wagons and pursuing Confederates, giving Minie Ball Hill its name. Lead bullets ("minie balls") are still found along the road where they were discarded in 1864.[75] It is likely then that Hayes, in his role as wagon-master, oversaw the jettisoning of those supplies.

From Salt Pond Mountain into West Virginia, the taxed brigades of the Kanawha Division encountered several more days of rain and crossed two large, flooded rivers. Exacerbated, Hayes captured in his journal the frustration of moving through such trying circumstances when he wrote "marched in driving rain over execrable roads…. The question is, can the train pass over such roads?"[76] The Kanawha Division remained in West Virginia for a few weeks before returning to Virginia in early June to join General David Hunter's raid on the railroad at Lynchburg, another component of Grant's orders for 1864 (see page 49).

Wind Rock Hike

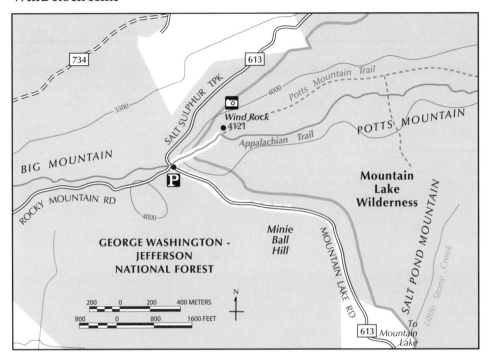

Distance: 0.5 mile round trip
Difficulty: Easy
Trailhead parking: From U.S. 460, turn northward onto Va. 613, also called Salt Sulphur Turnpike or Mountain Lake Road. In six miles, pass the turn-off for the Mountain Lake resort. Continue another five miles, pass over unmarked Minie Ball Hill, and continue 0.5 mile to reach a large parking lot where the A.T. intersects the height of this road. Ample parking is available in the lot, although parking should be limited to day-use. (Overnight parking is not recommended, since vandalism has been reported here.)
Description: A trailside information kiosk is located at the southern entrance to the trail. From the parking area, cross over the gravel turnpike to follow the A.T. north for a quarter-mile to reach Wind Rock. Time spent at the overlook offers an excellent opportunity to consider the road conditions you experienced in your vehicle compared to the arduous and muddy terrain faced by the troops who passed this way. The long-range views from Wind Rock over the valley and the ridge of Peters Mountain offer a perspective on the path of the Union return to West Virginia; their struggles didn't conclude when they reached the top of this 4,100-foot ridge. Complete the hike by returning on the same trail south to the parking area.
Other Activities: With this short hike complete, consider walking the half-mile southeast on the turnpike to Minie Ball Hill. Please remember that the lands on either side of Va. 613 are USDA Forest Service property, and the eastern side is part of the Mountain Lake Wilderness, protected areas. *Do not take any minie balls you may find along the roadside.*

You might also consider visiting Mountain Lake Conservancy and Hotel to see one of only two natural lakes in Virginia, to walk an easy trail around the lake, or to play Frisbee-golf. The hotel, scene of two Appalachian Trail Conference membership meetings in the 20th century, also was the site at which indoor scenes for the 1987 movie "Dirty Dancing" were filmed. You won't find Baby in a corner.

More information about the trail in this area, along with more history of nearby points, can be found in the *Appalachian Trail Guide to Central Virginia,* available at the Ultimate Appalachian Trail Store* (*www.atctrailstore.org*).

Activity in the Valley: Armies Cross Over the Future Appalachian Trail

The Shenandoah Valley was a valuable region during the Civil War. Control of the valley provided access to the abundance of the land—salt, iron, copper, and agricultural produce. The valley was also the thoroughfare—north and south, east and west using mountain passes—through which wagon trains and railroad lines passed, carrying vital supplies, as well as routes for regiments of men going to and retreating from battles. In fact, control in the valley spilled over into control of other fronts, ensuring the movement of armies and necessary supplies, so attention frequently was diverted to this arena to destabilize other fronts.

Stonewall Jackson's Valley Campaign of 1862

Confederate General Thomas J. "Stonewall" Jackson planned his strategy to control the valley in late April 1862. By May, he proceeded with his plan by traveling east with 5,000 infantry to cross over the Blue Ridge at Browns Gap. This effectively "threw Federal forces off his track,"[77] whether because they lost sight of him in the valley or were aware of his eastward movement and presumed he was headed to Richmond as reinforcement. The move allowed him to return, unsuspected, through Rockfish Gap near Waynesboro on trains bound for Staunton. There, he enlarged his force by 3,000 with the addition of Major General Edward "Allegheny" Johnson's men. They engaged with General Robert H. Milroy's troops in McDowell and continued on to Franklin, where they chased off Major General John C. Frémont before they returned to Staunton and headed north to Harrisonburg and farther down the valley.

In the valley campaign of 1862, three gaps now part of the Appalachian Trail were important to the Confederates' gaining control of the valley. Browns Gap and Rockfish

Stonewall Jackson. (Library of Congress)

View looking toward the Shenandoah Valley from Swift Run Gap. (Photo by Leanna Joyner)

Gap were passes through which Jackson himself crossed with his troops. Meanwhile, General Richard S. Ewell encamped at Swift Run Gap with roughly 8,000 troops, watching U.S. Major General Nathaniel P. Banks' activity in the valley and awaiting Jackson's return from forays in McDowell and Franklin. Then, on May 22, Ewell joined Jackson for the next part of the action. They bluffed movement down the central valley roads, while a main column, cloaked by Massanutten Mountain, surprised Federal troops to easily capture Front Royal on May 23.[78] Soon afterward, they took Winchester to push Major General Nathaniel P. Banks and his troops back toward the Potomac River not far from Harpers Ferry on the West Virginia/Maryland/Virginia borders.[79]

Jackson gained control of the Shenandoah Valley, exerted pressure on Washington, D.C., and threatened an invasion of the North. That precipitated the arrival of additional Federal troops into the valley and led to the second phase of the Shenandoah Valley campaign, which lasted until June 9, 1862.[80]

> Jackson also destroyed the Manassas Gap Railroad line, farther north in Virginia, as part of the 1862 valley campaign. See page 62 for the history of Manassas Gap in the Civil War.

Swift Run Gap and Browns Gap are now in Shenandoah National Park, and Rockfish Gap amounts to the southern boundary of the park and its Skyline Drive and the northern end of the Blue Ridge Parkway. Browns Gap is no longer a passable on a road, so it is most advantageous to visit it within the park and experience its new role as an east-west *foot* thoroughfare.

Swift Run Gap to Hightop Mountain Hike

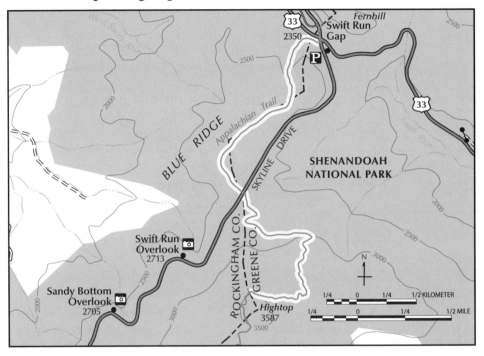

Distance: 3 miles round trip

Difficulty: Moderate

Trailhead directions: Arrive at Hightop Mountain parking area by traveling north or south on Skyline Drive through Shenandoah National Park or east or west along U.S. 33. Just south of Swift Run Gap's junction with U.S. 33 is the parking area.

Description: From the parking area, walk cross Skyline Drive to pick up the Appalachian Trail on the eastern side of the road (look for diamonds mounted on posts) and follow it southbound. The 850-foot ascent of Hightop Mountain is most pronounced for the next mile; the last half-mile to the summit is a bit more gradual. Two sets of open ledges on the western side of the summit afford views to the west and south; although the woods are considerably more grown up today, this provides a nice look at the long-range views afforded to the troops who held Swift Run Gap. Spend a few minutes there to consider the bulk of men and supplies that encamped at Swift Run Gap from late April until early May 1862. Ewell's 8,000 troops held this gap watching Federal activity in the valley and stood at the ready to either move east toward Richmond or west into the valley—whichever their orders dictated. Less than 0.1 mile from the second rock outcropping, a trail marker indicates your arrival at the wooded summit. Be sure to congratulate yourself for taking this hike; you just topped the highest point in the southern district of Shenandoah National Park. Return to the parking area by retracing your steps.

Browns Gap Loop Hike

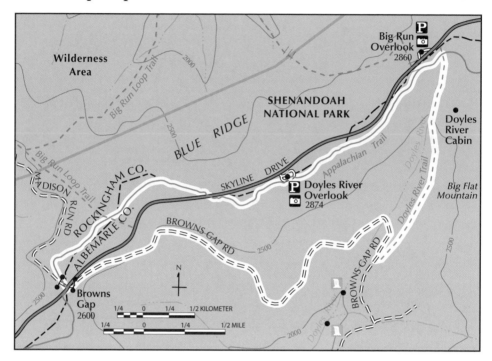

Distance: 4.8 miles round trip
Difficulty: Easy to moderate
Trailhead directions: Park at the Doyles River Overlook parking area, near milepost 81 along Skyline Drive in Shenandoah National Park.
Description: The hike begins on the southern side of the parking area. Pick up the path beside a kiosk to reach a junction with the Appalachian Trail, and turn right to walk south along a relatively flat section that parallels Skyline Drive. In 0.9 mile, pass through the Doyles River Overlook and, 0.4 mile later, cross over to the western side of Skyline Drive, continuing south on the Trail. In 0.9 mile, reach Browns Gap at Skyline Drive and a fairly obscure four-way trail intersection. The A.T. north and south intersects with Madison Run Road heading west and Browns Gap Road heading east. As you approach the parking area for Browns Gap, Madison Run Road is to your right and slightly behind you (at the western corner of the parking area). Walk to Skyline Drive and identify Browns Gap Road on the northeast diagonal from the parking area. Take Browns Gap Road through a gate. Begin a gentle descent along the road. In 0.4 mile, a short side trail on your left leads to the grave of William H. Howard, Co. F of the 44th Virginia Infantry, C.S.A. You are traveling in Stonewall Jackson's footprints now as you forge down this road on an eastward traverse. Hike 1.4 more miles on Browns Gap Road to reach a junction with Doyles River Trail, and make a left on that trail to begin a slightly taxing ascent of the Doyles River drainage on the side of Little Flat Mountain. In 0.8 mile, reach the intersection with the Appalachian Trail and the Doyles River Overlook parking area.

Hunter's Raid: 1864

The second primary activity that occurred in the central part of the Shenandoah Valley during the war was "Hunter's Raid." During the raid, a crisscrossing pattern of forces traveling east and west over the Blue Ridge Mountains deeply intertwines the story of this military action with the location of the A.T. today.

Ulysses Grant's effort to strain the resources of the Confederacy and cut railroad supply lines resulted in General George Crook's and Brigadier General William W. Averill's raid on the Virginia and Tennessee Railroad in May 1864 (see page 40). Just after that action, General David Hunter, newly assigned to lead the West Virginia forces, was assigned to control the valley and dismantle the railroads that

benefited the Confederates. (Slightly more than a year later, General Hunter would be commanding the pallbearers who guarded Abraham Lincoln's casket on its long trip home to Illinois.)

The first action of this campaign began with a Federal victory in Piedmont on June 5. By the evening of June 10, Hunter was just north of Lexington and gained Crook and Averill's forces as reinforcements.

On June 10, a detachment led by General Alfred N. "Nattie" Duffié had departed from Hunter's main column near Staunton and traveled east to Waynesboro before splitting into two groups—one proceeded to Rockfish Gap, and the other traveled southward along the western slopes of the Appalachian ridge to cross to the east at

Maj. Gen. David Hunter. (Library of Congress)

the Tye River gap. The gaps now intersect the Appalachian Trail at I-64 and Va. 56, respectively. Between June 7 and 10, Confederates held Rockfish Gap, but the June 10 advance of Duffié's troops, along with knowledge that Lexington had fallen to the Union, intimidated Confederates into an eastward retreat.[81] On June 11, Federals occupied Lexington and burned Virginia Military Institute (VMI).

On June 11, VMI cadets left Lexington along the James River to "defend Balcony Falls" and "camped on the Blue Ridge some two miles from Balcony Falls,"[82] likely very close to today's Trail. The A.T. crossing of the James River near Va. 501 intersects with the course of cadets determined to defend through this pass any quest for Lynchburg.

Meanwhile, on the eastern side of the Appalachian range, Duffié's detachment went to Arrington Depot with a mission to sever the rail line between Lynchburg and Charlottesville, although they ultimately failed in that assignment. Duffié received orders from Hunter to reconvene with the army in Lexington "by the most practicable route and with as little delay as possible." So, Duffié crossed over Whites Gap[83]—where present-day U.S. 60 intersects the Blue Ridge Parkway, a few miles west of the U.S. 60 trailhead known as Long Mountain Wayside in A.T. guidebooks. According to Richard Duncan in *Lee's Endangered Left: The Civil War in Western Virginia, Spring 1864*, and his official reports to his commanders, Duffié's brigades encountered two sets of Confederate troops on their westward movement before they stopped and spent the night in Whites Gap.

> ## Hike Whites Gap
>
> A suggested hike originating from Whites Gap/Long Mountain Wayside can be found in the section on Brown Mountain Creek at the conclusion of this book.

By June 13, Hunter received the supply train he had been awaiting. On the same day, Duffié's men arrived in Lexington, and another group of Federal cavalry was on an eastward route through Whites Gap toward Amherst Court House. [84]

On June 14, Hunter's army departed Lexington in pursuit of Confederate troops led by General John A. McCausland, Jr., a former VMI cadet who at age 16 guarded John Brown after his trial in Charles Town. McCausland delayed the Federals' advance on Lynchburg by personally setting fire to the bridge over the James River in Buchanan, much as he had done to try to protect VMI in Lexington by torching one over the Maury River—then known as North River. McCausland's men also created obstacles on the steep road leading east from Buchanan to the crest of the Blue Ridge. They felled trees, blew up narrow portions of the road with gunpowder, and even used nature's power of erosion by diverting streams to flow on to it, carrying away sediment and creating a muddy mess.[85] Near the top of the ridge, the armies passed through Bearwallow Gap; the Appalachian Trail now crosses their path. With just a bit more elevation gain, the Federal troops took the 2,000-foot ridge and encamped on the night of June 15. The next day, Union troops continued down the eastern slopes of the mountains to the town of Bedford and then north to the Battle of Lynchburg that occurred on June 18.

Confederate forces under General John C. Breckinridge, former vice president of the United States, were poised in Lynchburg by June 15, realizing that Hunter's aim was to destroy the critical Southern transportation hub, host to the Kanawha Canal as well as two train lines—the Orange and Alexandria and the Virginia and Tennessee. Confederate reinforcements continued to arrive in Lynchburg through the morning of June 18, some by foot and others by train, passing through Rockfish Gap. General Jubal Early realized Confederates were outnumbered for battle

Union troops repair a section of the Orange & Alexandria Railroad. (Library of Congress)

and staged a ruse by running empty trains back and forth over the James River to create the illusion they had more reinforcements arriving.[86] A member of the 23rd Ohio recorded in his diary on June 17 that he "could hear trains arriving, bands playing and thought by the sound troops were marching from the depot to the works in front of us."[87]

At Lynchburg, Hunter incorrectly assessed the power of the Confederate troops to be more than his own 18,000. In actuality, they had just 14,000. Assuming he was outnumbered, he retreated. Pursued by Confederates for the next few days, Hunter's regiments were pummeled again at Hanging Rock, near Salem, on June 21 in a narrow notch created by a river nestled between mountains. Those who escaped that attack proceeded west, over what is today Va. 311 below Catawba Mountain, the top of which hosts the iconic McAfee Knob and the A.T. Finally, they reached the Catawba Valley, no longer pursued by Rebels, and were able to rest.

> After General Early's raid on Washington (see page 70), he returned to upper Virginia and skirmished with General Crook's cavalry at Snickers Gap, along the Appalachian Trail just south of Harpers Ferry. A suggested hike for Snickers Gap is included in the chapter on northern Virginia.

Hunter's next move left the Shenandoah Valley undefended. He led his troops farther west to New Castle and then into West Virginia. That provided the Confederates the opportunity to move north through the valley into Maryland and to the outskirts of Washington, D.C., menacing the North and forcing a diversion of Union troops from the battlefields of Richmond and Petersburg toward the mountains of Virginia and the Potomac Valley once again.

McAfee Knob Hike

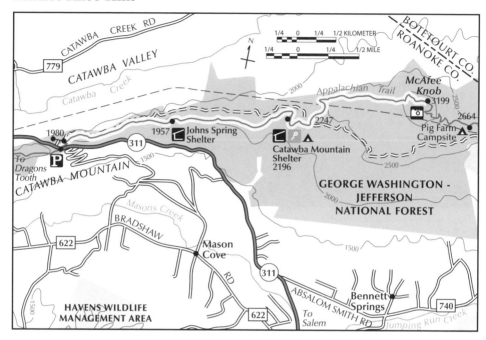

Distance: 7.4 miles round trip

Difficulty: Moderate

Trailhead directions: Going south on I-81 from Salem, Va., take the exit for Va. 311, and proceed a short distance to the junction with Va. 311 on your right. Drive five miles to reach the height of the Catawba Mountain pass. As you approach the large trailhead parking area on the left, you will pass signs warning of pedestrians crossing the road.

View from McAfee Knob. (Photo by Leanna Joyner)

Description: The trail to McAfee Knob begins just across Va. 311 from the parking area. Ascend the embankment, and begin a steady climb for 0.2 mile to a trailside kiosk. The gently graded trail undulates for the next couple of miles. Several dry bridges over slanted bedrock make the footing a bit easier for portions of this first section. You will pass two A.T. shelters, both on your right as you approach the summit. After passing the second shelter, the trail begins a more significant incline, first crossing over a gravel road, then becoming steeper the closer you get to the top. Shortly, you reach a modest blue-blazed path and a sign indicating the viewpoint of the knob. The relatively odd outcropping and sweeping panoramas offered from this overlook make it one of the most photographed places on the Appalachian Trail. From here, you have a clear view right down into Catawba Valley where Hunter's men were finally able to rest, no longer pursued by Confederates. **Other activities**: Either on the approach to, or just following, this hike, consider a visit to the site of the Hanging Rock Battle, in which McCausland soundly rousted Hunter. Just five miles north up Va. 311 to Salem from the A.T. trailhead parking area, it is an easy addition to the day hike. Another rewarding Appalachian Trail hike is a 16.8-mile round trip hike from the parking lot south to Dragons Tooth. From the tooth, you can see more views of Catawba Valley as well as the eastern fork of the Blue Ridge that hosts the parkway and the Peaks of Otter, above where Hunter's troops originally passed through on the way to Lynchburg.

Peaks of Otter and Sharp Top Overlooks Hike

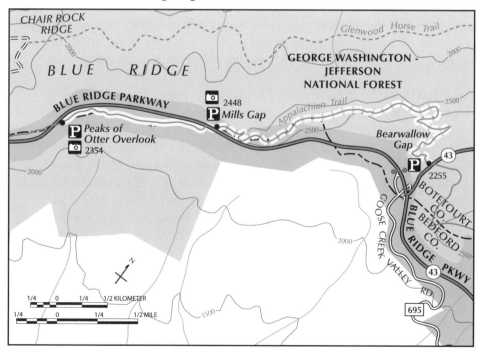

Distance: 1.4 miles or longer round trip

Difficulty: Easy

Trailhead directions: Park at Blue Ridge Parkway milepost 92.5 at the Peaks of Otter Overlook, located on the parkway south of its southern junction with Va. 43, east of Buchanan off I-81.

Description: This hike offers an excellent way to experience the majesty of the central Blue Ridge without too much exertion. If you can schedule your hike in mid- or late June, you will be rewarded with rhododendron in bloom, just as the soldiers were in 1864. Begin this easy hike by identifying the white-paint blazes marking the Appalachian Trail on the northern end of the parking area. The northbound trail parallels the parkway for 0.7 mile along the top of the ridge to Mills Gap Overlook. The view from Mills Gap Overlook includes shimmering glimpses of the James River in the valley below and a recollection of the role it played during this installment of the Civil War. You can conclude your hike by returning the way you came on the trail, or you can continue on 1.7 miles to the A.T.'s intersection with Bearwallow Gap. If you decide to carry on to Bearwallow Gap, the reward will be found under the canopy rather than at overlooks, so appreciate the minutiae of the color of the leaves, crawling bugs, blooming wildflowers, and relative quiet, since you'll be a bit farther from the sounds of the parkway. Conclude the longer version of this hike by retracing your steps.

Rockfish Gap: Final Blows in 1865

The location of the 200-mile, Richmond-to-Covington Virginia Central Railroad and the Blue Ridge Tunnel through Rockfish Gap guaranteed frequent passages of troops through this singular pass on the future A.T. in central Virginia. It played prominently in the movement of troops in Jackson's valley campaign of 1862 and in Hunter's raid on Lynchburg in 1864. Final blows reached the gap in 1865.

Following Hunter's retreat from the Shenandoah Valley, General Grant sent General Philip H. Sheridan and 45,000 men to squash Confederate General Jubal Early once and for all. His orders included the instruction to "strip the valley itself so thoroughly that 'crows flying over it for the balance of the season will have to carry their provender.'"[88] Between September 19, 1864, and March 2, 1865, Sheridan and Early fought battle after battle, eventually coming to a final clash at Waynesboro on March 3, in which Sheridan drove the Confederates out of the valley completely[89]—sending them in retreat over Rockfish Gap for the final time. Roughly a month later, General Robert E. Lee surrendered to Grant at Appomattox Courthouse, 65 miles to the south.

More information about the trail in this area, along with more history of nearby points, can be found in the *Appalachian Trail Guide to Central Virginia* and the *Appalachian Trail Guide to Shenandoah National Park,* available at the Ultimate Appalachian Trail Store* (*www.atctrailstore.org*).

Action in Northern Virginia

Between Chester Gap, east of Front Royal and just north of Shenandoah National Park, and Harpers Ferry, a peninsula/panhandle of West Virginia dividing Virginia from Maryland, is a fifty-three-mile segment of the Appalachian Trail. More than six decades before this section of the A.T. was blazed, this land was visited on numerous occasions by the armies of the Union and the Confederacy—moving offensively and defensively. This area was a hotbed of activity between 1861 and 1865 with frequent troop movements, skirmishes, and efforts to control each other's communications and supply lines.

The Appalachian Trail in northern Virginia travels the spine of the Appalachian ridge through territory once called "Mosby's Confederacy." This territory was under the watchful eye of John Singleton Mosby and his Partisan Rangers, as well

continued on page 61

Soldiers of Company A, 22nd New York State Militia, at Harpers Ferry in 1862. (Historic Photo Collection, Harpers Ferry NHP)

Hikers on the Appalachian Trail often assume trail names, nicknames that represent personality or would-be persona or a quirk. John Singleton Mosby roamed the Appalachian Trail before it was a trail, yet he still managed to garner something akin to a trail name. The Gray Ghost, as he was called, was a mysterious and illusive Confederate soldier renowned for his cunning and impudence.

Just 27 years old at the start of the war, the Gray Ghost was slight in stature at 5'7" but considerable in spirit. His blue, "keen, reckless eyes" could assess people and situations swiftly, leaving him "cool in danger, quick to think and practical in carrying out his ideas."[90]

Early in his military career, he performed a few services for the Confederacy that set the tone for the remainder of his enlistment—bold actions, sneak attacks, and intelligence about the enemy's force and movements.

By early 1862, Mosby developed a friendship with future General J.E.B. Stuart and began acting as an aide to him. In March of that year, Mosby was sent to discover if the Union pursuit of Rebel General Joseph E. Johnston, former quartermaster general of the U.S. Army, was a legitimate threat or a distraction. Mosby's ride around the

John Singleton Mosby. (Library of Congress)

enemy revealed that the small Union force in pursuit of Johnston was small and isolated. In fact, Mosby discovered that the larger force had already retreated and left only "a curtain of cavalry." Armed with that information, Stuart pursued the Federal cavalry and captured 30 prisoners, 16 horses, and some arms.[91] That was the first of Mosby's scouting trips he recounted in his autobiography; the next, in early June 1862, was heralded with more fanfare since it led to Stuart's ride around General George B. McClellan, still general-in-chief of the Union army.

That early June, Mosby went on a preliminary scouting trip for Stuart to gain information requested by commanding General Robert E. Lee. Stuart, relying on Mosby's information, took 1,200 cavalry and two pieces of artillery and began to ride around McClellan in northern Virginia. Mosby said it was he who "conceived and demonstrated that it was practicable. I took four men… and went down among the Yankees and found out how it could be done."[92] Stuart's sweep around McClellan took 48 hours of continuous riding, brought the Confederates within five or six miles of the McClellan's headquarters, revealed the weakness of his right flank, and provided details on the Federals' supply line. Lee used this information to take advantage of Union weaknesses and sever the supply line during the Seven Days Battle, unraveling the U.S. campaign in the peninsula.[93] More than the vital information it provided the Confederate leadership, it was an embarrassment for the paralyzed Union military under McClellan.

The unprecedented circuit around the Federals was a unique tactic that Mosby continued to hone as he used surprise to catch his opponents off-guard.

On July 19, less than a month after the ride around McClellan, Mosby was captured. During his ten-day detainment, he managed to charm his captors as well as surreptitiously gain information about McClellan's intended movements. With an awareness of the Federal military strategy, Mosby gained his freedom during a prisoner exchange and rushed to Lee to personally deliver the information. Lee forwarded news of General Ambrose E. Burnside's movements to General Stonewall Jackson, and Jackson responded by striking generals Nathaniel P. Banks and John Pope at Cedar Mountain before Burnside's reinforcements could arrive.[94]

Mosby showed that, by gaining a precise awareness of the enemy's location and intentions, the Confederates could strike first to disarm, scatter, and defeat the Federals. He considered securing information and intercepting communications of vital importance to the Confederate cause, and that was key to his own success in northern Virginia.

Colonel Mosby's most notorious and romanticized activities took place early in his career, but the legendary boldness that characterized them shone in other reconnaissance missions and future raids.

Following Lee's invasion of Maryland and the Battle of Antietam/Sharpsburg in September 1862, Mosby recruited a small group of men, fifteen to start, in January 1863 to begin partisan activities in northern Virginia. Mosby's purpose was to reclaim control of supply lines abandoned a year earlier by Joe Johnston.[95] He also meant to "compel the defense of Washington" by emphasizing the continual presence of Confederates so close to the capital.

As he worked toward those goals, his command quickly grew. With thirty partisans, Mosby carried out one of his most extraordinary escapades of the war—the capture of "brigadier general" Edwin H. Stoughton (his appointment had expired), two captains, thirty privates, and fifty-eight horses at Fairfax County Courthouse on

Fort Corcoran was one of several Union defenseworks around Washington, D.C. (Library of Congress)

March 23, 1863, all without an injury or loss to himself or his men. That raid as well as a few other heroic incidents led to his promotion to major of the Partisan Rangers in April 1863. As Mosby's popularity increased, so did his enlistments.

James Williamson, one of Mosby's original recruits, recounted the appeal of the Mosby battalion to new recruits in his book, *Mosby's Rangers*:

> *Men came from all over the country to join him [Mosby].... Although a dangerous service, there was a fascination in the life of a Ranger; the changing scenes, the wild adventure, and even the dangers themselves exerted a seductive influence which attracted many to the side of the dashing partisan chief.*[96]

Between January 1863 and April 1865, as many as 1,900 enlisted to serve as Partisan Rangers in the 43rd Virginia.[97] The life of a Partisan Ranger with Mosby was a coveted position. In fact, Mosby was required to verify that new recruits to his regiment were not deserters from other posts.[98]

Partisans lived in their own homes or in the farmhouses of hosts scattered throughout Fauquier and Loudoun counties, the northernmost Virginia counties to be grazed by the future A.T.[99] They gathered only by notice for specific purposes, disturbing Federal supply lines or intercepting communications.

Mosby's Rangers were the only guerillas sanctioned by General Lee, who felt that bands operating as rangers had potential to deteriorate to crime. He respected the actions of Mosby and his leadership of the Rangers and found his service indispensible.[100] To retain the credibility of soldiers enlisted in the 43rd, membership cards were issued to separate the legitimate Mosby Rangers from impostors seeking to use guerilla tactics to their own benefit.

To further protect the reputation of the Rangers, Mosby established boundaries for his battalion. The northern and southern boundaries are now gaps along the Appalachian Trail. Mosby's men were to remain when not on duty within the boundaries of Snickers Gap (Va. 7 east of Berryville) at the northern end and Manassas Gap (Va. 55 near Linden) at the southern.[101] The area consists of roughly 125 square miles of land[102] and now contains 26 miles of the Appalachian Trail. The term "Mosby's Confederacy" is used more loosely now, to include the areas that he and his men dominated. They displayed intimate familiarity with the terrain and had alliances with local residents.

His greatest responsibility in northern Virginia was to weaken the enemy by requiring U.S. commands to stay in upper Virginia to protect their interests in railroads and communications. His signature was surprise. His presence was a nuisance to the Union and a strain on their resources.

Throughout 1863, Mosby and his men operated frequently east of the Blue Ridge. Following the losing Gettysburg campaign, Mosby was required to turn his attention more fully to northern Virginia, where a lot of Union regiments were stationed to secure the gaps in the Appalachian range. Mosby's "Rangers gnawed at the edges of the Federal units, apprehending stragglers and patrols, and targeted wagon trains for attack."[103]

In 1864, the protracted battle for the Shenandoah Valley shone a spotlight on the critical role that Mosby's Rangers could play to reinforce Confederate opportunities and thwart Union aspirations.

Throughout the year, he and his men ransacked camps of Federals, stalked wagon trains of supplies, derailed entire trains and robbed them of goods and passengers, and intercepted or cut Union communications. Many of those actions took place near the A.T. route or required crossing over the future trail. A night raid on a sleeping encampment of Federal troops at Loudoun Heights above the Potomac River opposite Harpers Ferry, a raid on a wagon at Berryville west of Snickers Gap, the so-called Greenback raid in which the Rangers derailed a Union train and made off with $173,000 in Federal payroll on October 14, 1864, and an engagement with General Duffié at Ashby Gap (on U.S. 50)—all are part today of the historical lore lacing the Appalachian Trail in northern Virginia.

By mid-August 1864, Union generals Sheridan and Grant had devised a plan to drive Mosby and his men out of northern Virginia. It included "total destruction of all private rights in the country occupied by such parties."[104] Captain Richard Blazer and a company of "Independent Scouts" were assigned the sole task of "cleaning out Mosby's gang."[105]

Throughout the fall of 1864, newspapers followed the pursuit of Mosby by reporting "attacks by Mosby, followed by hunts for Mosby, escapes by Mosby, and rumors about Mosby."[106]

Characterized by loyal Southerners as Robin Hoods[107] and by Union soldiers as criminal guerillas, Mosby and his men were revered and feared, blessed and cursed, protected by members of the community, and hunted by Blazer and his men.

During the hunt for Mosby, seven of his men captured during an engagement with Federals at Chester Gap were later executed in Front Royal under orders from General George A. Custer. The brutal and illegal act of war led in November 1864 to a "measure-for-measure" retribution by Mosby, who chose seven Union prisoners by lot but eventually had only three hanged. Two who were shot survived.

One of his most valued Rangers throughout 1864 was Lewis T. Powell, a large 19-year-old at the time who in January 1865, using the alias Lewis Paine, had joined in John Wilkes Booth's conspiracy to kill Abraham Lincoln. Powell's assignment was to kill Secretary of State William H. Seward, and for that failed attempt he was hanged in July 1865.

Mosby was sought many times but never captured during his later years as a Ranger, although he was wounded nearly mortally on December 21, 1864. The Rangers eventually beat Blazer and his scouts in November 1864. Mosby's promotion to colonel came the following month. They disbanded in Salem weeks after Lee's surrender but never formally surrendered themselves. Later, General Grant paroled Mosby, who later served his former antagonist as a lawyer and campaign advisor, which earned Mosby violent enmity among his Virginia neighbors.

The Appalachian Trail of today between Chester Gap (U.S. 522 east of Front Royal) and Harpers Ferry in West Virginia on the Potomac is where the Gray Ghost's rich history lives on.

$\sim$

as his informants in the surrounding communities (see page 56). He was charged primarily with disrupting the supply and communications lines of the Union. That he did unfailingly. He robbed wagon trains of supplies, derailed entire trains of goods and passengers and cash, and ransacked camps of Federals.

Between 1861 and the end of 1862, most of the activity in the gaps consisted of troop movements for the reinforcement of armies fighting at Manassas/Bull Run or for the tug of war over the Shenandoah Valley.

In 1863, following the Battle of Gettysburg, Federals pursued General Robert E. Lee back into Virginia and began a systematic effort to control the gaps in the Appalachian ridge—including Chester, Manassas, and Ashby. Some were held more successfully than others.

With the establishment of Mosby's Rangers in 1863, this territory was under closer scrutiny and was more heavily guarded by Confederates until the end of the war. While both Federals and Confederates used the gaps of the Appalachians as thoroughfares to eastern or western destinations, domination of the gaps generally was retained by Mosby's band of guerillas, who closely watched movements of Federals and struck whenever opportunity presented itself.

> When [Mosby's] Rangers rode toward the Shenandoah Valley, they usually crossed at one of four gaps—Chester, Manassas, toward Front Royal; Ashby's on the road to Winchester; and Snicker's, toward Berryville. The Rebels favored the Snicker's Gap route more and more as the campaign unfolded because, at Berryville, they could canter westward to Winchester or northward to Charles Town, Harpers Ferry, and the Baltimore & Ohio Railroad.[108]

The following examples of the Blue Ridge actions show the frequency of military passages through the gaps, although an accurate four-year count cannot be calculated. These forays were critical to the success and failure of campaigns elsewhere; messages or supplies intercepted in transit could doom a mission. In fact, in 1864, considerable conflict occurred throughout these gaps as both sides fought to control the valley. Movement through the gaps subsided in early 1865 because much of the Shenandoah Valley and its resources had been stripped by Federal forces, leaving them only their hunt for Mosby and his men until the war's end that April.

Chester Gap/Front Royal

After the Gettysburg campaign, Confederate troops held Chester Gap. U.S. Colonel William Gamble led the First Division, Cavalry Corps, of the Army of the Potomac, to Chester Gap in an attempt to occupy it. In the gap, Gamble's men skirmished with General George E. Pickett's men before falling back. The follow-

View of Front Royal, Virginia from the Skyline Drive. (© Can Stock Photo)

ing day, July 22, 1863, the Confederates advanced, Gamble fell back again, and the Confederates maintained control of the gap.[109]

More than a year later, on September 23, 1864, Union troops were encamped at Chester Gap. The next day, seeking to surprise the group but mistaking its size, Mosby's men led by captains William H. Chapman and Walter E. Frankland attacked the rear and the front of the brigade, but Mosby's men had engaged too large a force. Those in the rear realized the size of the regiment almost immediately and quickly fell back to Chester Gap; those under Frankland skirmished in the front and drove the Federals back toward the gap.[110] Suddenly, more Federals appeared, cutting off the line of retreat for Chapman. According to Ranger James Williamson's later account, fifteen or twenty Federals were killed, along with two Confederates.[111] Seven of Mosby's men were captured and later executed in Front Royal—an uncharacteristic fate for prisoners of war. The order was made by "Boy General" George A. Custer. A note pinned to one of the executed said this would be the fate of any of Mosby's men who were captured. The executions set the stage for retaliation by Mosby in November (see page 60).

Manassas Gap/Linden

The Valley Campaign of 1862, led by Confederate General Thomas "Stonewall" Jackson, marked the destruction of the Manassas Gap Railroad from Thoroughfare Gap to the east and Strasburg to the west. A brief feint by the Federals to rebuild the line in September 1864 never went beyond an engineer's examination.[112]

Linden was a common rendezvous point for Mosby's Raiders. The town, now just a mile from the Appalachian Trail crossing at Manassas Gap (Va. 55), also marked the southern boundary of "Mosby's Confederacy."[113]

On May 15, 1862, Confederate cavalry attacked a Union wagon train passing through Manassas Gap and Linden; all but three of the seventeen troops guarding the wagon train were taken prisoner.[114]

The first week of November 1862, U.S. General William W. Averill encountered Rebels "at the mouth of Manassas Gap, and drove them back into the pass, where they took up position supported by artillery."[115]

A brigade of U.S. cavalry was sent to occupy the gap following the Battle of Gettysburg. They retained control while other Federal forces pushed toward Front Royal. Skirmishing occurred here on July 21 and 23, 1863, but the Union retained its stronghold in the gap.[116]

On May 28, 1864, Mosby and 144 men passed by Linden and camped just short of Front Royal. The next day, they continued into the Shenandoah Valley as reinforcements for Confederate defenses against Hunter's raid in the valley (see page 49).[117]

Hike to Mosby Campsite

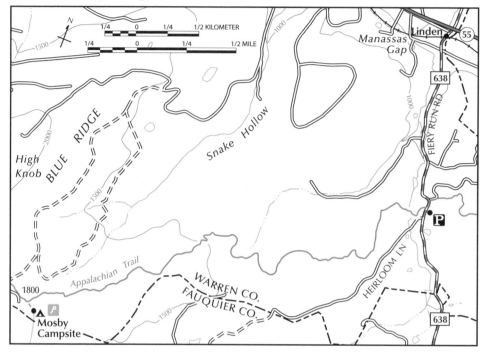

Distance: 8.6 miles round trip

Difficulty: Moderate

Trailhead directions: Travel on Va. 55 to reach the town of Linden, Virginia. At the intersection with Va. 638, Fiery Run Road, turn right, if arriving from the west; left, if arriving from the east. Travel south-southeast on Va. 638 about one mile to reach an eight-space parking area at the trail intersection.

Description: Given the proximity of Manassas and Chester gaps to one another, this hike captures the lure of both locations. The "Mosby Campsite" that marks the destination for this hike is not one likely to have been used by Mosby and his men, but the Potomac Appalachian Trail Club (PATC) named a shelter here in his honor after its construction in 1939.[118] The shelter was stolen in 1980 for its chestnut logs,[119] and, since that time, it has been called Mosby Campsite, with water provided by Tom Sealock Spring.

Begin the hike from the parking area by traveling south on the Appalachian Trail, toward the Jim and Molly Denton Shelter and Chester Gap/U.S. 522. The first mile provides a gradual gain in elevation to the Denton Shelter, found on a sunny knoll and offering an ample porch to rest, if necessary. Alternately, hikers may opt to take advantage of the shelter's welcoming appearance and seats on the return portion of this hike.

Continuing south, the path ambles along the slope to gain 500 feet of elevation over the next mile and passes beneath a powerline. A short distance farther is a junction to the east with a blue-blazed side trail to Mosby Campsite and Tom Sealock Spring. (Sealock was a Fauquier County farmer who became a Ranger in 1863. Following the war, he lived in Linden and was buried near Manassas Gap.[120])

While this hike does not offer sweeping vistas or broad rivers, it offers the chance for reflections on the land Mosby loved and knew well, land he and his men looked after and, some say, still do.[121]

Once you have considered the Gray Ghost and his reign over northern Virginia, follow your own footsteps, and those who have been here before you, to return to Fiery Run Road and your vehicle.

Other Activities: Follow up on the hike and the capture of Mosby's men in Chester Gap by traveling to Front Royal. In the Prospect Hill Cemetery, the bodies of the men Custer executed were laid to rest. Front Royal also offers Civil War Trails' interpretive markers at other sites throughout the town. Other activities to consider include canoeing, rafting, or tubing on the Shenandoah River *via* one of the many local outfitters.

Ashby Gap

The more northern gaps in Virginia—Ashby and Snickers Gap—are known for the most frequent passages over the Appalachian Ridge during the Civil War. The reliance on these gaps was due to their proximity to Harpers Ferry, Manassas, and Washington, D.C. The landscape also allowed the easiest passage over the mountain range at these two gaps.

Furthermore, Paris, just a mile from the Appalachian Trail crossing at Ashby Gap, was a common meeting place for Mosby's Partisan Rangers. These men likely crossed the gap to gather, then crossed through the gap again in pursuance of orders.

One of the most notable crossings of Ashby Gap was July 19-20, 1861. Here "Stonewall" Jackson allowed his weary Rebel soldiers to rest before resuming a march at dawn to arrive in time for the first Battle of Manassas/Bull Run.[122] A historical marker at the gap commemorates this event, but it was just the beginning of Civil War military use of this pass, which might also have featured in Revolutionary War (and earlier) campaigns.

In September 1862, a Confederate wagon train passed through the gap, and a Federal detachment was sent to capture or destroy it. Near the gap, a Union charge startled Confederates, who scampered into the woods and through the gap, but very little of the wagon train was captured or destroyed.[123]

As General Lee was moving into Maryland to begin what became the Gettysburg campaign, his General J.E.B. Stuart fell back to Ashby Gap on June 21, 1863, after "furious fighting" with Union cavalry in Upperville.[124] Following Gettysburg, Union troops took control of the gap on July 20, 1863.[125]

Operations in the valley that began in the summer of 1864 resulted in frequent passages over Ashby Gap. The months from July to December account for the majority of the them by Mosby and his men, as well as by U.S. troops hoping to suppress or eliminate Confederate raids. Specifically, generals Philip Sheridan and Ulysses Grant had ordered counteroperations against Mosby and his men in September. They called for the destruction of private property in an effort to clean out Mosby and his gang from northern Virginia and said that the "county should not be capable of subsisting a hostile army."[126]

On July 19, 1864, General Alfred N. Duffié's Union cavalry passed through the gap and skirmished with the enemy before they moved on to Berry's Ford. That evening, they fell back to the gap. That night, Mosby's Rangers engaged the Union troops under Duffié and captured roughly 50 men, as well as horses, guns, and supplies.[127]

Seven of Mosby's men had been captured and executed in Front Royal in September. In retribution for this action, Mosby's men imposed a similar fate on Union soldiers in early November 1864. (See page 60.) The Federals were captured east of the Blue Ridge and executed not too far from Winchester. Mosby's men traveled with those prisoners over the ridge at Ashby Gap before carrying out an execution "measure for measure," as had been done to their comrades, although only three were actually killed in the end.[128] After the hangings, Mosby sent letters to the Federal leadership to implore them to let this be the last uncivilized deaths of the war, and the leaders agreed.

Around that same time, Federals persisted in raiding the private property of residents of Fauquier and Loudoun counties. A cavalry effort led by Colonel William Powell raided Manassas Gap and continued on to Markham, Piedmont, Rectortown, Upperville, and Paris. They collected all the horses, cattle, and stock that they found as they swept through the country and then returned with their bounty through Ashby Gap on November 9 to a Federal camp on the west side of the ridge.[129]

Partisan Ranger Richard Montjoy and Company D of Mosby's 43rd Virginia Brigade were in Paris on November 15, 1864. From there, they moved to Berryville. Along the way, they skirmished with Union troops, captured seventeen, and gained some horses. When they were closer to Berryville, they were attacked by another set of Federals, this time led by Captain Richard Blazer, who had the express mission of routing out all of Mosby's men. Company D fared poorly, losing all they had captured earlier. One of Montjoy's company was killed, and four or five others were injured, one mortally.[130]

Roughly two weeks after the Blazer victory, Union General Wesley Merritt passed through Ashby Gap on November 28 with the task of laying waste to even more

View along the Appalachian Trail south of Ashby Gap. (Photo by Leanna Joyner)

of the countryside in order to drive out Mosby's men.[131] The Union focus on the elimination of Mosby's band was as unwavering as Mosby's persistent attacks on Federals over the past two years.

The Federals' efforts to force Mosby and his men from Fauquier and Loudoun counties continued into the following year. Major Thomas Gibson and 250 men searched homes and farms for Mosby, his men, and his supplies. By February 19, 1865, Gibson's command had been split. The troops with him had captured 18 prisoners and about 50 horses. Up to this point, Gibson had fought off small bands of the enemy, but, when he left Paris for Ashby Gap, a Confederate attack from forty rangers led by Dolly Richards significantly damaged his brigade. Gibson lost everything he had captured, including the prisoners, and suffered the capture of his men and 90 horses.[132]

The incidents above are just a few illustrations of passages common through this territory that included scrapping battles between men; the capture and recapture of prisoners, supplies, and horses; and a continuous struggle to control the roadways and turnpikes of Ashby and Snickers gaps.

Even with Lee's imminent surrender to Grant at Appomattox Courthouse in early April 1865, Mosby and his men continued to persevere in their quest for military control of northern Virginia. On April 8, Mosby himself passed through Ashby Gap on his way to scout around Upperville. This turned out to be his last scouting effort of the war and may have been his final passage through this gap in official military service to the Confederacy.[133]

Signal Knob Hike

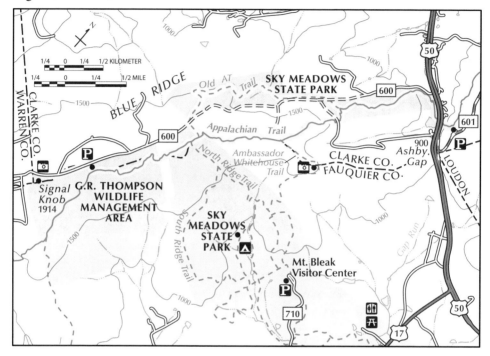

Distance: 7.3 miles; shorter options available

Difficulty: Moderate

Trailhead directions: Approaching Ashby Gap from the west, either from Winchester or I-81, take Exit 281A to U.S. 50/17 East. Travel roughly 9 miles along a divided highway, passing a historical marker commemorating John Singleton Mosby and his Partisan Raiders. After 9 miles, begin looking for signs indicating Va. 601; the turn will be on the left and will also be signed Blue Ridge Mountain Road. Proceed 0.2 mile and keep close watch on the left-hand side of the road for an inconspicuous entrance for trailhead parking, marked by a small brown sign.

Description: From the trailhead parking lot, the spur trail leads down 0.1 mile to a junction with the Appalachian Trail. Turn left, and head south on the trail to return to U.S. 50. Cross the four-lane highway carefully. After you cross, you will see a historical marker commemorating the site of Jackson's camp and Mosby's activity. Ashby Gap proper is a short distance uphill, to the left. Return to the trail to enter the woods, passing remnants of historical stone walls as you parallel U.S. 50. Cross a small creek, and then veer south to ascend in a moderate climb. Reach a junction with the old trail in 1.1 mile. Stay left on the A.T., and soon cross over a grassy road.

Enter a clearing on the woodland's edge. This section of the A.T. was relocated by PATC in 2005 to offer variety from the forest canopy. For the purpose of revisiting history, the clearings are also more accurate historically, as many ridges were cleared in the 19th century for farming as well as for furnace fuel. The next couple of miles are through relatively open areas.

Imagine as you walk through the open area how much quieter it would be to move through fields rather than on roads with the clip-clop of horses' hooves. While Mosby and his men moved along roads for speed, they took to fields and forests to move with stealth.[134]

In 0.7 mile, reach another open area and encounter a junction with the Ambassador/Whitehouse Trail. A viewing area a short distance along the Ambassador Trail provides vistas to the east toward Paris. Consider enjoying a picnic and relaxing for a while. If you chose, you can conclude your hike now, by returning the way you came, for a 4.2-mile hike, or continuing another 0.7 mile along the ridge to a junction with the Old Trail. Following that trail back to its northern intersection with the A.T. and back to your vehicle makes a 6.1-mile hike.

Hikers pushing on toward Signal Knob will continue past the Ambassador Trail along the ridge, pass through a gate in a wire fence, and reach a junction with the Old Trail on the right. Continue on the Appalachian Trail to come to a bench and the North Ridge Trail in a young forest, marking three miles of foot travel from the trailhead parking lot.

The A.T. used to cross the crest of Signal Knob but has been relocated to the eastern slope of the knob. The remaining portion of the hike to reach Signal Knob is an easy half-mile walk near the ridge. Signal Knob no longer offers the vistas it offered early A.T. hikers or the clear views it provided when it served as a signal station during the war in the 1860s. The forest has taken hold again and obscures the view, but visitors can still sense in glimpses through trees the long-range perspective this observation point offered.

According to a 1934 guidebook published by the Potomac Appalachian Trail Club, Signal Knob provided an "extensive view in all directions from this point: east over Piedmont Valley with Manassas/Bull Run Mountains in distance; south to several high peaks; southwest to another Signal Knob at northern end of Massanutten Range; west beyond Shenandoah Valley, the eastern front of the Alleghenies may be distinguished on a clear day. The Blue Ridge sprawls in a northeasterly direction toward Harpers Ferry." The guide also says that a soldiers' cemetery is located on the east slope of the ridge, although, if it is close to the A.T.'s current location, it remains unmarked.

Despite limited views, hikers wishing to experience Signal Knob, in homage to the role this site played as a signal station for both Union and Confederate forces during the war, will continue south on the Appalachian Trail to a spur trail on the right. The junction is denoted with a pictogram for camping, and the trail leads 0.1 mile past a couple of campsites before reaching a trailhead kiosk and a boundary road for the wildlife-management area. Turn left, south, on the boundary road, uphill for 200 feet, and gaze east over the ever-growing trees and shrubs toward the Manassas hills. This limited view is all that's offered from Signal Knob these days.

Finalize your hike by returning the way you arrived. Upon reaching the junction with the Old Trail, take a left to follow the forested Old Trail 1.9 mile to the Appalachian Trail. **Other Activities:** Visit scenic Sky Meadows State Park. In addition to offering 12.8 miles of beautiful hiking trails, the park also is the site of a historical home that once served as a safe house used by Mosby's men. The estate, known as Mount Bleak, was a 171-acre farm later sold to former Mosby Ranger George M. Slater. Primitive, hike-in campsites are also available in the park.

Snickers Gap

In addition to being a frequent thoroughfare for Federal and Confederate troops, Snickers Gap also marked the northern territory for "Mosby's Confederacy."

Snickers Gap must have been covered by thousands of troops hundreds of times, from both sides, during the course of the war.

On May 5, 1863, a trap was set by the 67th Pennsylvania led by Colonel John F. Staunton to capture Mosby and his men, but the plan backfired when the Federal troops fired on their own men in haste.[135]

When the Confederates defeated the Union forces at Lynchburg and drove them toward West Virginia, General Jubal Early was given the opportunity by General

Jubal Early. (Library of Congress)

Lee to move Confederate forces through Harpers Ferry into Maryland and to menace Washington, D.C. Before Early could cross into Maryland there, Union troops discovered his movements and from Maryland Heights destroyed the bridges across the Potomac. The Rebel commander had to regroup and cross upriver at Shepherdstown, but his momentum was lost. Early's raid on Washington was brief but caused enough panic that Federal reinforcements were diverted to drive him away. He returned toward the valley through Snickers Gap on July 16, 1864, when he encountered a Federal force led by General George Crook. Early and Crook clashed again on the 18th at Cool Spring along the Shenandoah River below and west of Snickers Gap near Berryville.

A historical marker in the gap is located on the northern side of Va. 7, closest to the westbound lanes, but the actual battle site is slightly northwest on riverside lands below the A.T. now protected by the Appalachian Trail Conservancy.

Mosby Ranger James Williamson in his memoir reported several seemingly innocuous passages over Snickers Gap on July 20 and 31 and August 20, 1864, that do not correlate with other significant Confederate activity, although the trips must have provided certain value at the time—either to scout or otherwise menace or track Federal troops and supplies. [136]

View looking southwest from Bears Den Rocks near Snickers Gap. (Photo by Leanna Joyner)

Relatively close to the Appalachian Trail in Berryville, Mosby orchestrated an attack on a U.S. supply train on August 12, 1864. The attack, commonly called the Berryville Wagon Train Raid, began when Mosby and 300 of his men passed through Snickers Gap heading west toward Berryville.[137] Upon encountering the train of 525 wagons bound for General Philip H. Sheridan in the Shenandoah Valley, Mosby struck. He reported having destroyed 75 wagons and securing more than five hundred horses and mules.[138] A formal inquiry into the events revealed that he debilitated the rear of the wagon train, destroying only twenty of the "back fifty" wagons, and captured only two hundred and fifty horses and mules.[139] The immense discrepancy is difficult to reconcile, but this is one of the successes of Mosby's career that certainly led to his notoriety. It may be that the profound victory he reported was the basis for the screenplay that later took the stage called "The Guerrilla; or, Mosby in Five Hundred Sutler-wagons."[140]

Shortly after the Berryville raid, U.S. generals William T. Sherman and Ulysses S. Grant set their intentions to capture or kill Mosby and disband his men. On September 3, Mosby and 90 of his men were camped on the ridge at Snickers Gap. They had stopped early because of heavy rain. The next morning, they traveled to Myers' Ford on the Shenandoah below the current A.T. in the Shannondale area of Jefferson County, West Virginia. As Mosby and fifteen others were away scouting, the remaining 75 men were ambushed by Captain Richard Blazer as they lounged in the woods. Thirteen were killed, six wounded, and five captured. Blazer's scouts beat Mosby's men severely by using their own Ranger tactics—intelligence as to their location and a deft surprise attack. The ambush sent Confederates breaking and scattering in all directions; one died and five others were wounded. [141] (Three months later, a detachment of Mosby's men captured or killed all but two of Blazer's scouts in a fight near Kabletown, West Virginia, to the west.)

On September 15, four hundred Union cavalry swept along the flanks of the Blue Ridge, capturing prisoners, cattle, and wares. They rode all day in high temperatures to reach Snickers Gap. While they rested, they were attacked by fifty to eighty of Mosby's men under the leadership of Captain William H. Chapman. Mosby himself was not present at this engagement, having been injured the previous day by a gunshot wound to his thigh. Mosby described Chapman's heroics in this way: "Captain Chapman soon came plunging down the mountainside like an avalanche and was firing among the men before they were awake. They had not expected an enemy to come like a bolt from the sky, and the attack caused a general stampede."[142] The shock of Chapman's attack was likely due to his unexpected course of travel. He had traversed the spine of the Appalachian ridge from Ashby Gap to Snickers Gap along a mountain road, which sounds strikingly close to the course of the Appalachian Trail today. (Va. 601, Blue Ridge Mountain Road, today connects the two gaps and parallels the A.T.)

Mosby's memoir of the incidents of September 15 suggests that this attack may have been the Union impetus to execute his men in Front Royal following their capture at Chester Gap (see page 61).[143]

In October, Mosby and his men derailed an eight-car Baltimore & Ohio passenger train eleven miles west of Harpers Ferry at Quincy's Siding in present-day Bardane. They began by cutting telegraph lines along the path, then disrupted the tracks to create the derailment. Their most significant gain of this action was finding Federal paymasters onboard the train. They took the $173,000 in "greenbacks," robbed the 200 passengers of $20,000 in cash, set fire to the train, and left.[144] They ended the raid on October 14 as they had begun it on October 13, by crossing over the ridge at Snickers Gap. They arrived from the east and returned from the west—with their pockets more full of money.[145] The track was operational by the following day, and this small nuisance to the Union forces was likely one of the more ineffectual raids Mosby's men undertook.[146]

At the end of the war, Mosby formed Company H, Mosby's Cavalry Regiment, and, on April 6, 1985, under Captain George Baylor, it made one last foray out of Snickers Gap, across the Shenandoah, following it downstream until the Rebels came across Union cavalry at what is now called Millville, killing two, wounding four, and taking 65 men and 81 horses prisoner.

Bears Den Rocks—Snickers Gap Loop Hike

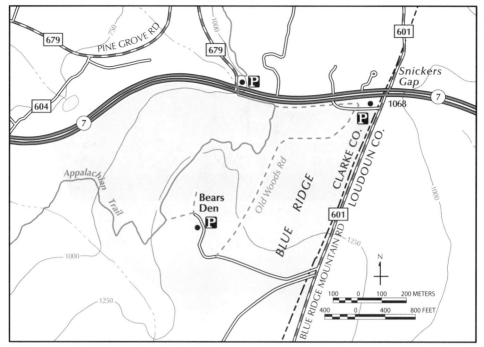

Distance: 1.4 miles

Difficulty: Easy-to-moderate

Trailhead directions: There are two available parking areas for this hike. The first option for a very short hike, or if you decide to enjoy this hike late in the day, is to park at the Appalachian Trail Conservancy's Bears Den property, managed as a hostel by the Potomac Appalachian Trail Club. Hikers may park in the lower lot for a daily fee. Reach Bears Den by turning south onto Va. 601 from its intersection in Snickers Gap with Va. 7 and travel 0.3 mile to 18292 Blue Ridge Mountain Road; the driveway is on the right. The mailbox post has an Appalachian National Scenic Trail emblem that will help ensure you are at the right place.

The second option is a commuter lot located on the corner of Va. 7 at Blue Ridge Mountain Road/Va. 601. If arriving from Winchester, Berryville, or other points west, you will see a historical marker indicating the Appalachian Trail and Bears Den. This land-mark indicates you that you are approaching Blue Ridge Mountain Road, and the parking area is on your right. You need to watch closely for the turn-in. If arriving on Va. 7 from Round Hill, Purcellville, or other points east, approach the height of land, and turn left on Va. 601, then make an immediate right into the parking lot.

Description: This description originates from Bears Den, the first option above. Hikers beginning at the commuter lot (north on the A.T. 0.6 mile) should adjust the description to their hike.

Beginning at the lower parking lot at Bears Den, walk up the lane farther until you are beyond the Bears Den Hostel building and in another small parking area. Make a left on

View looking northwest from Bears Den Rocks. (Photo by Leanna Joyner)

the blue-blazed trail indicating the route to Bears Den Rocks. It is a short and easy hike to the rocks, which rewards you with views of the Clarke County countryside, the Shenandoah River, and, on a clear day, as far west as Berryville.

From this perspective, you can imagine the land below with fewer trees, more farms, and many ferry crossings of the Shenandoah, rather than the few bridges of today. The hike will take you from this overlook point to Snickers Gap before looping back up to your vehicle.

Mosby's men traveled from Snickers Gap to Berryville where they struck the Union wagon train. Following the raid, Ranger Williamson described the mood in this way:

> *Our men were wild with excitement and elated with their success, gave vent to their feelings with shouts and yells and merry songs, the braying mules and lowing cattle joined in the chorus"*[147]

The hoots, shouts, and songs of victorious soldiers likely gathered in the valley and rolled up the hillsides much like the sounds of moving cars and trucks now heard from the highway below.

From Bears Den Rocks, return back on the spur trail a few steps to the junction with the white-blazed Appalachian Trail. Turn left on the Appalachian Trail, and continue easily along the gradually descending path. After reaching a large cluster of boulders on your right, the trail drops a bit more significantly down some well-placed steps. The trail intersects with a blue-blazed side trail leading to the commuter parking lot at Va. 7; an interpretive sign installed by local middle-school students is also located at this junction.

Continue to follow the white-blazed Appalachian Trail north to reach Snickers Gap at Va. 7, slightly west of the parking area. From this intersection with the road, the A.T. crosses diagonally northwest to continue toward Harpers Ferry. But, to conclude this loop hike, turn right along the shoulder of Va. 7 and stay as far as possible from the fast-moving traffic of this busy, divided, four-lane highway. (Some hikers prefer to walk inside the guardrail.) In less than 0.2 mile, reach the commuter parking lot and the alternate start location for this hike.

From the commuter parking lot, identify an inconspicuous side trail along the wooded, southern side of the lot. After a few steps along the trail, blue blazes on the trees confirm that you are on the right track. Continue to pick your way through rocks along the path to reach a faint four-way junction under a small power line. A few steps farther is a relatively well-worn path on the left; follow the unmarked path a few hundred feet to a sign indicating that you are on the Old Woods Road. (An alternate to returning to the parking area at Bears Den is to continue on the blue-blazed trail to its junction with the A.T. at the interpretive sign, and return along the Appalachian Trail south to Bears Den Rocks).

The Old Woods Road begins with a mild climb that becomes a bit steeper the closer you come to the parking area at Bears Den. Along the road, you will pass a side trail to a cabin at Bears Den that is available to rent through the hostel. As the trail levels out, it also splits; take the route on the right, under the power lines, to arrive at the parking area.

A rewarding way to experience this hike may be late in the day. If you decide to conclude the hike at Bears Den Rocks at dusk, be sure to bring a headlamp to guide you back to your vehicle. From the overlook, you will see the electric lights in the valley below, but one can think of the sparse lighting of lanterns in far-off residences of the 1860s. If the moon isn't too full, you can watch the stars reveal themselves as you capture the experience of evenings at camp—watching for approaching enemies and taking in the elements: fresh air, breeze, snow, rain, or a cloudless, star-filled sky.

More information about the trail in this area, along with more history of nearby points, can be found in the *Appalachian Trail Guide to Maryland–Northern Virginia,* available at the Ultimate Appalachian Trail Store* (*www.atctrailstore.org*).

"*National Signal Station on Loudoun [sic] Heights, Harper's Ferry, Communicating with the station on Maryland Heights. Sketched by our special artist.*" From Frank Leslie's Illustrated News, November 8, 1862. (Historic Photo Collection, Harpers Ferry NHP)

Loudoun Heights

Loudoun Heights above Harpers Ferry and the southern shore of the Potomac River has several memorable stories associated with the Civil War—including the first would-be destination of John Brown's aborted freedom campaign, the defense and fall of Harpers Ferry throughout the war, and a mysterious tale of a cave used by Confederate Raider John Mosby as a hide-out.

Had John Brown's raid been met with success on its southerly freedom campaign, Loudoun Heights would have been the first mountain fastness in which he and his colony would have sought refuge from pursuers. It would have been from Loudoun Heights that attacks into densely slave populated northern Virginia counties would have been made. While the heights of this Virginia land may have been part of Brown's strategy, his fall in the armory engine house (see page 88) ended his campaign and his dream of liberation for Southern slaves.

As Harpers Ferry changed hands throughout the course of the war, so did the heights of Maryland and Virginia. The posts of these heights and their commanding views provided the defenses—and offenses—critical to military occupation of the low-lying town. Rarely did Confederate or Union control of Harpers Ferry abandon posts that overlooked the ferry, for to do so would increase the opportunity for attack that would topple control of the transportation and communications hub that Harpers Ferry was in those days.

As early as May 1861, Loudoun Heights was secured to protect Harpers Ferry. General Thomas "Stonewall" Jackson ordered the construction of blockhouses on the heights during the Confederate control of Harpers Ferry between April and June 1861.[148] Shortly after their construction, Jackson's comrade, General Joseph Johnston, determined Harpers Ferry to be indefensible, abandoning the town and the heights. The town itself increasingly became deserted after the armory and arsenal were burned, removing most of the jobs—what growth it had in those years came from fugitive slaves seeking refuge behind Union lines.

The subsequent Federal control of Harpers Ferry was a bit more *laissez faire* in its management of the heights. In fact, in 1862, the largest capitulation of Federal troops to a Confederate invasion was due in part to the lack of defenses on Loudoun Heights. On September 13, 1862, General John G. Walker (CSA) met no Federal resistance on his arrival at Loudoun Heights.[149] From here, the fortifications sometimes visible today from the town's heights during the depth of winter, he commanded a view of Harpers Ferry and a clear shot at the town with the five rifled cannons his men and horses or mules heaved up to the 1,180-foot summit. Most exposed was what is known today as Camp Hill, then full of tents and now the site of a quarter-mile blue-blazed trail connecting the A.T. on the Shenandoah River side of the hill to Appalachian Trail Conservancy headquarters along the town's main street. The rifled cannons were in place by 10 a.m. on September 14, and the men began firing by 1 p.m.

This undefended post allowed Confederates, attacking from the south (General A.P. Hill) and the west (Jackson) in three prongs, to oust Federals from their positions in Harpers Ferry on September 15. On that date, 12,500 newly recruited troops under Colonel Dixon S. Miles—fatally wounded while approaching the surrender ground—succumbed to Jackson on Bolivar Heights at the west end of the adjacent towns of Harpers Ferry and Bolivar, site of a four-hour battle almost a year earlier. This conquest provided the Confederate invasion into Maryland with supplies from Harpers Ferry and control of transportation and communications lines, as well as a reasonable escape route back into Virginia.

Lasting just a couple of days, Walker's control of Loudoun Heights covered the Potomac and the Shenandoah rivers, the town at their confluence, and the Baltimore & Ohio Railroad tracks on the northern shore of the Potomac just inside

Ruins of the Harpers Ferry Armory, photographed by Alexander Gardner in July 1865. Maryland Heights is on the left, Loudoun Heights is on the right. (National Archives)

View of Harpers Ferry from Loudoun Heights, showing the confluence of the Potomac (right) and Shenandoah rivers. (Photo by David T. Gilbert)

Maryland. From here, Confederates exhibited their dominance, raining down fire on the town from the southeast as well as from the northern shore of Maryland Heights. This pressure, in tandem with that of Stonewall Jackson's approach from the west across Schoolhouse Ridge, blocked Federal troops from any potential escape and sealed their surrender.

Following the Maryland campaign's disastrous end at Antietam/Sharpsburg and the Confederates' abandonment of Harpers Ferry, the town was once again taken up by the Union and more or less continuously held by Federals through the end of the war. During the first several months of resuming control of Harpers Ferry and Loudoun Heights, a division of the Army of the Potomac built a military road, stone redoubts, and a signal station atop Loudoun Heights.[150]

Fifteen months later, on a midwinter night heavy with snow, Loudoun Heights was center stage for a famous clash between Confederate Rangers led by John S. Mosby and an encampment of Maryland cavalry. On January 10, 1864, Mosby and his men, operating under intelligence from a highly respected scout of General J.E.B. Stuart, approached a Union camp on Loudoun Heights. Arriving stealthily through the snow, Mosby's men surrounded the First Potomac Home Brigade, Maryland Cavalry, at 4:30 a.m. and noted "not a sentinel awake."

The scout, Benjamin Franklin Stringfellow, was given the honor of descending on the camp's headquarters to capture Major Henry Cole. Instead of following the instructions, Stringfellow and a few others rushed in, whopping and firing their guns, awakening the sleeping Union soldiers, and causing Mosby to mistake his own men for the enemy. This started an exchange of gunfire, initially among Mosby's own men and then with the awakened Union cavalry, many who hadn't time to dress before the exchange.

One of Cole's Marylanders shared the petrified terror that must have pulsed through the men at camp before they sprang into action: "No one who has experienced a night attack from an enemy can form the slightest conception of the feelings of being awakened in the dead of night with the din of shots and yells coming from those thirsting for your blood."[151]

The blunder of mistaken identities produced mixed results for the Confederates, rather than a complete victory. In the end, Mosby gained sixty horses and six prisoners, and his men inflicted twenty-six casualties on the First Potomac Home Brigade. Mosby's Raiders suffered fourteen.[152]

Some speculate that the debacle of this night raid was a turning point in Mosby's leadership and that he never again felt comfortable carrying out night attacks.[153]

While the story of Mosby's attack on the sleeping camp of Marylanders is a well-documented and infamous tale of the 43rd Virginia Battalion, a lesser-known and more speculative connection between Mosby and Loudoun Heights appears in the literature. This aspect of Loudoun Heights is not included in A.T. guidebooks or Harpers Ferry National Historical Park guides, most likely because it is difficult to know if it is true. According to one account, caves dot the shore of the north-flowing Shenandoah River along the cliffs of Loudoun Heights. The author of those accounts brilliantly describes the mysterious disappearance of Mosby and his raiders on two occasions and later details the discovery of the cave, capable of hiding as many as two hundred horses.[154] The only written source about the supposed cave is not acknowledged or substantiated by Harpers Ferry National Historical Park, suggesting that it may be that this fanciful description has only served to enhance the mystique of John S. Mosby and is more romantic fodder for the legend of the Gray Ghost.

Loudoun Heights Hike

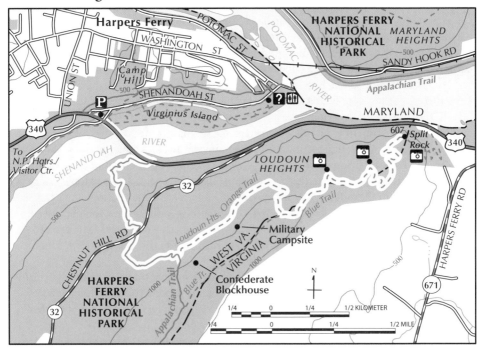

Distance: 4.6 miles round trip

Difficulty: Moderate

Trailhead parking: The most ideal parking for this hike is in a lot near the intersection of Shenandoah Street and U.S. 340 along the Shenandoah River on the southeast corner of Harpers Ferry. If parking is not available, parking with shuttle service delivery to this location is available at the main Harpers Ferry National Historical Park entrance on the south side of U.S. 340, at the top of the hill about 1.25 miles from the bridge over the river. Parking at either location costs $6 per vehicle, and the fee covers three consecutive days. With this in mind, hikers would probably plan to hike Loudoun Heights one day, climb Maryland Heights one day, and spend another day exploring Harpers Ferry and Virginius Island.

Description: Begin this hike where Shenandoah Street and U.S. 340 meet. Follow the Appalachian Trail 0.3 mile over the Shenandoah River on the pedestrian portion of the bridge. At the end of the bridge, the walkway curves around, descending steps to pass under the bridge, before beginning a moderate climb of 0.4 mile to cross over W.Va. 32 (Chestnut Hill Road). The Trail is steeper until it reaches Loudoun Heights. In 0.2 mile, the trail parallels an old charcoal road and shortly crosses over the gullied old road at the site of an old charcoal hearth.

The deep charcoal road is a reminder of just how barren this slope would have been during the Civil War. Historian and author David Gilbert in his book, *A Walker's Guide to Harpers Ferry,* suggests that the road was built sometime after 1827. It provided access to 2,000 wagonloads of trees that were converted into charcoal each year.[155] Leading up to the

Civil War, the area was home to nine charcoal hearths—flattened semicircle or elliptical areas where wood was carefully stacked and slowly burned to create the charcoal necessary to fuel the forges of the iron and other industries on the shore below.

Since the road was an established route to the crest of the heights, it was likely used by Confederates in the construction of the blockhouse in 1861 and again in September 1862 to haul the five rifled cannons to the summit for their seizure of Harpers Ferry (see page 78). The road may have been further improved by Federals who took up more permanent patrol of the heights between the fall of 1862 and the conclusion of the war.[156]

The last half-mile to reach the junction with the Loudoun Heights Trail and the top of the ridge is the last appreciable climb of this hike. The Appalachian Trail southbound turns to the right at the junction; take a left at the junction to continue your hike on the Loudoun Heights Trail or what's now known as the Orange Trail.

Look carefully along this section for the remains of the blockhouse built by Stonewall Jackson's Confederate troops in the spring of 1861. Visitors can also find rock redoubts and stone foundations that were the base of camp huts. Thirty-five stone redoubts were built by Federals in the fall of 1862, along with rifle pits, a log signal station, and camps.[157] The best time to visit the heights to glimpse the remains is in the winter, spring, and summer. The heavy foliage of the crest that releases a colorful array of leaves to the ground in the fall does obscure the identification of these historic sites but makes a rewarding treasure hunt for history buffs and young children.

Amble along the crest for another 1.4 mile to reach a short side trail to your left that leads to rocky outcrops beneath a power line. The outcrop offers commanding views of Harpers Ferry, Bolivar, and the confluence of the two great rivers. This is one of the few chances to gain the perspective of an unimpeded gaze offered the soldiers of the war.

The wide rocks of the outcrop offer an excellent place for an extended break and mark the halfway point, 2.3 miles, of the journey. Return the way you arrived, noticing any minutia of the landscape, the fortifications, or the trail that seem different approaching from the other direction.

More information about the trail in this area, along with more history of nearby points, can be found in the *Appalachian Trail Guide to Maryland–Northern Virginia,* available at the Ultimate Appalachian Trail Store˚ (*www.atctrailstore.org*).

Harpers Ferry from Maryland Heights. (Photo by Leanna Joyner)

Harpers Ferry

Harpers Ferry is a gateway to the Appalachian Trail, the nexus of what John Brown called The Great Black Way, and one keystone to the war strategies of Union and Confederate armies along the broad dividing line between North and South.

Harpers Ferry is rich in history, and much of the town now is under the protection and management of the Department of the Interior as the Harpers Ferry National Historical Park. The Appalachian Trail offers the chance to hike through the abundant history of this storied landscape.

Harpers Ferry, Then and Now

Harpers Ferry was designated first as a national monument in 1944 and became a national historical park in 1963. Since that time, the town has been gently massaged to look partly like it did in 1859, so that visitors can step easily into the history of the place. While there are many things that are exactly the same, and others that closely resemble the way things were, the contrasts are more pronounced, especially in the landscape, both natural and built, since many of the military buildings were buried years after being torched during the war, and floods removed others.

Back then, Harpers Ferry was more densely populated. "The Point" at the confluence of the two rivers that now serves as an ideal viewing spot of the waters and the mountains to the east, north, and south was replete with homes and shops. At least 3,000 people lived in Harpers Ferry in 1859[158], compared to slightly more than 300 today.[159] They worked at the factories in town and on Virginius Island just offshore in the Shenandoah. Cotton and pulp mills, a rifle factory, a machine shop, a blacksmith shop, a carriage factory, the iron foundry, the arsenal, and the armory all gave the town a bustling appearance in old lithographs. In 1859, the U.S. armory alone employed 400 people.[160]

The dense population and the industry were largely reliant on surrounding woodlands to make the charcoal that fueled iron furnaces and blacksmith forges. That created a dramatic and detrimental impact on the surrounding mountains. The environmental degradation of the slopes surrounding Harpers Ferry was severe. The heights around Harpers Ferry that are now full of trees and wildlife were barren in the mid-19th century. The land was denuded of trees to make charcoal. It is estimated that two thousand wagonloads of trees were removed from just Loudoun Heights each year between 1827 and 1859.[161] As many as six times that much might have been removed from Maryland Heights, and the other woodlands of the county to the west became as equally depleted. Charcoal-makers were working as fast as possible to feed the unquenchable fuel requirements of the pulsing growth of industry.

Charcoal was created by stacking wood on flat, semicircular hearths and burning it slowly by restricting oxygen to the smoldering timber by covering it with dirt. Loudoun Heights had nine of these hearths, and Maryland Heights had fifty-seven. Once the charcoal was made, it was transported to nearby Keep Tryst, Blue Ridge, or Antietam Ironworks,[162] where it was used to smelt iron that was used to make any number of household items, tools, weapons, and machines.

The removal of timber from the slopes of Loudoun Heights and Maryland Heights provided a clear line of sight from nearly any point on either of the heights, across the two rivers and the town below to the other heights. Now, one must hike to just the right spot on rocky outcroppings of either to see the commanding view of the town and rivers one would have had in the years during the Civil War.

Changes to the landscape and the town occurred throughout the course of the war, too. Certainly, the town did not look the same after the war as it did in 1859. It was blown up with explosives, set on fire, ravaged by regiments, isolated, occupied, besieged, abandoned, ramshackled, and rebuilt more than once throughout the course of the war. The bridge over the Potomac, for example, was destroyed and rebuilt nine times during the four years of fighting.[163]

Harpers Ferry, circa 1859. The covered bridge across the Potomac River was burned by Confederate troops in the first weeks of the Civil War. (Historic Photo Collection, Harpers Ferry NHP)

Starting in 1859, two years before the war began and not ending until 1865 with Robert E. Lee's surrender of the Confederacy at Appomattox Courthouse, Harpers Ferry was occupied almost continuously as a vital resource—a link in the land that figuratively separated the North and the South.

At first, the town was a pivotal point for the resources for war, arms and ammunition. Harpers Ferry had been home to the arsenal and armory since 1799 and, as a result, was an objective to control. As the war progressed, Harpers Ferry became a keystone to the war, because it was a hub of transportation and communications. For the Union in particular, maintaining the railroad lines east to Washington and west to Ohio ensured the mobility of troops and supplies to the western fronts. The Confederacy set their sights on Harpers Ferry a few times during the war for supplies and to shield the Shenandoah Valley, as well as to secure a route of retreat for its northern invasions.

That briefly describes this tiny town in the period leading up to and during the Civil War. This hamlet that sits between two big rivers and is watched over by the heights of Virginia and Maryland has its fair share of stories through which we can walk as we meander along the Appalachian Trail.

John Brown and the Great Black Way

Harpers Ferry was the site of John Brown's raid, viewed as a precursor to the Civil War not so much because of its failed audacity but because it ignited panic among the slaveholding South.

John Brown was a fervent abolitionist from the Midwest, where he had engaged in no small amount of blood-letting, who had sworn to fight for the cause of freedom and equality, and he did just that on October 16, 1859. He believed that the nation needed to be shaken[164] out of complacency to a directed consciousness of slavery and its evils and toward its abolition.

John Brown. (Historic Photo Collection, Harpers Ferry NHP)

John Brown perceived Harpers Ferry as the gateway to "The Great Black Way," the safest way for slaves to travel to freedom. It marked the clearest route for escape and the most solid hope for protection in the face of a battle to incite freedom. The strategy Brown crafted envisioned utilizing the Appalachian ridges[165] and mountains south of Harpers Ferry as forts and "hiding places easily capable of becoming permanent fortified refuges for organized bands of determined armed men."[166] From those posts, he and his army of ever-increasing freed or escaped slaves could fight for the cause. They would begin their attacks into the densely slave-populated Fauquier County, Virginia,[167] to liberate slaves, and retreat with increased numbers to the mountains. There, hiding in a "labyrinthical wilderness,"[168] he planned that they would arm new members of their band, then invade again, retreat, regroup, and repeat—on a southerly freedom campaign. (Fauquier County is more than 35 miles south of Harpers Ferry but was home to Dangerfield Newby, a free mulatto who was the first of the Brown raiders to be killed in Harpers Ferry.)

Just more than a year before the Secessionists drew up the Confederate Constitution, John Brown had drafted a constitution that would serve as the foundation for a "band of isolated people fighting for liberty" that he planned to lead in revolution.[169] The "Provisional Constitution and Ordinances for the People of the United States" would bind the raiders' organization in order to "avoid anarchy and confusion."[170] Based on the U.S. Constitution, *Brown's* Declaration of Independence addressed the rights of *all* citizens as free and independent. The document

John Brown's Fort sits adjacent to the Appalachian Trail in Lower Town Harpers Ferry. (Photo by David T. Gilbert)

sought to protect "persons, property, lives, and liberties" of its people. Beyond establishing rules of governance and parameters for military action and peace, the constitution mandated rules on property and labor and instruction on noble ways of living. It said that property and money are meant for common ownership to the benefit of the group rather than any individual. It restricted the needless destruction of property and the concealment of weapons—they were to be carried openly. It required labor by all, devotion to the Sabbath, the establishment of schools and churches, and respect for marriage and family.[171]

With this plan in mind, Brown and 19 men arrived in Harpers Ferry from the ridges of Maryland on the evening of Sunday, October 16, 1859.[172] They crossed over the Potomac River on the Baltimore & Ohio Railroad viaduct and bridge and easily took control of the arsenal without one shot fired. Also as peacefully, they secured access points and manned posts at the bridges and river crossings of the Potomac and Shenandoah rivers. That beginning concluded the relative calm that opened the insurrection.

Five miles away at the Kennedy farmhouse in Maryland, their gathering point over the previous few weeks, Brown had 2,000 rifles and 1,500 pikes. With the arsenal captured, he had control of more weapons and munitions. With the stockpiled weapons he had amassed, those would give his movement the "bang" necessary for the campaign ahead.

John Brown's "Fort"

The engine house that became John Brown's "Fort" now sits beside the Appalachian Trail 150 feet from its original 1848 location, which is buried under debris from tunnel-building. After being moved four times since 1891, it was finally reassembled in Lower Town in 1968 as close as possible to its historical location.

> **John Brown Exhibit**
> Visit the John Brown Exhibit in the John Unseld Building on Shenandoah Street, just across the street from the "fort."

After securing Harpers Ferry, six men went to round up the first of what Brown hoped would be many slaves and slave owners. They returned with 46-year-old Colonel Lewis Washington, Frederick the Great's sword and the Marquis de Lafayette's pistols (inherited from George Washington), and all of his male slaves from Beall-Air—Washington's plantation about six miles west along the railroad tracks. They also seized another planter, John Alstadt, and six of his slaves who lived much closer, at an old Lee-family house where all the hostages were held.[173] According to W.E.B. Du Bois's biography of Brown, by daybreak on Monday, October 17, twenty-five to fifty slaves were armed.[174] According to Alstadt's testimony, the slaves who were taken from him and Washington were armed with pikes to guard against the escape of their owners.[175] Things seemed to be going according to Brown's plan.

During the same period of time, an arriving Baltimore & Ohio passenger train pulled into Harpers Ferry and was temporarily detained. In the emotions of the moment, a freed-black baggage handler, Heyward Shepherd, was shot. With the first shot of the raid fired, train passengers and the town erupted with fear of this uprising. It was this panic that swept the nation as news of John Brown's brazen attack on Harpers Ferry was read in newspapers across the states in the days and weeks that followed.

Osborne Anderson, one of Brown's men, wrote in his published memoir of the event: "Men, women, and children forsook the place in great haste, climbing up hillsides, and scaling the mountains. The latter seemed to be alive with white fugitives, fleeing from their doomed city."[176]

Brown's hope to shake the nation into consciousness now in motion, he sent men back to the farmhouse in Maryland to retrieve stockpiled arms to be used with what was captured at the arsenal as they made their way across the Shenandoah and into the mountains to begin their freedom campaign. Unfortunately for Brown's dream, the supplies from Maryland never arrived.

*Marines storm the Armory fire engine house—John Brown's Fort—on October 18, 1859. The cap-
tion on this illustration, which appeared in the November 1859 issue of "Harper's Weekly," reads:
"The Harper's Ferry Insurrection. – The U.S. Marines storming the Engine-House. – Insurgents
firing through holes in the wall." (Historic Photo Collection, Harpers Ferry NHP)*

Oswald Garrison Villard wrote a biography of Brown in 1910 that questioned
multiple aspects of Brown's military strategy. Villard argued that a well-trained
military leader would have stowed arms for the fight in mountains south of Harpers Ferry or at least kept all his weapons with him, so that a quick attack of the
town would have been sufficient.[177] The supplies from Maryland were eventually
abandoned as the couriers learned that forces had arrived in Harpers Ferry to
squelch the uprising.

When Brown realized the delay of the arms, he selected a number of influential
hostages to be relocated with him and his men to the smallest of the three buildings in the arsenal compound along the Potomac. The engine house, now commonly called John Brown's Fort, was quickly adapted for the defensive position he
was forced to adopt. By 10 a.m. on October 17,[178] the angry residents of Harpers
Ferry, with aid from a Martinsburg militia, had started taking potshots at the
building and the hostages and captors within. Three of Brown's men were sent
out from the fort at two separate times with white flags to implore a ceasefire. The
first, William Thompson, was captured. In the second attempt, Brown's son was
shot and mortally wounded, and chief aide Aaron Dwight Stevens, 28, was taken
prisoner.

Throughout the day, the town's chaotic response to the insurrection was fueled by drunkenness.[179] At one point, unarmed Mayor Fontaine Beckham was shot and killed. In response, an angry mob grabbed captive Thompson and dragged him to the railroad bridge. They shot him in the head, threw his body in the river, and used it for "target practice."[180]

One of Brown's hostages recounted the scene: "In a few minutes, every window was shattered, and hundreds of balls came through the doors. These shots were answered from within whenever the attacking party could be seen. This was kept up most of the day, and strange to say, not a prisoner was hurt, although thousands of balls were imbedded in the walls, and holes shot in the doors almost large enough for a man to creep through."[181] The firing intensified from within and outside of the building as the day progressed before subsiding once night fell.

By dark, five of the men who had arrived with Brown were dead, and three others, including two of Brown's sons, were wounded and would later die of their injuries.[182] Five townspeople had been killed, and seven others wounded.[183]

Just before midnight on October 17, U.S. Lt. Colonel Robert E. Lee arrived with between 90 and 100 Marines. By daybreak on Tuesday, October 18, negotiations for the surrender of Brown and his men were rejected. The door was battered down on the second blow with a ladder used as a ram.[184] John Brown—pointed out to the Marines by Colonel Washington—and his conspirators were taken prisoner. Marine Private Luke Quinn, a 33-year-old Irish immigrant, was killed while storming the engine house. He was buried alongside what is now the Appalachian Trail on the hillside above the old armory site after a funeral in St. Peter's Catholic Church, which was saved from Civil War shelling because Father Michael Costello flew the British Union Jack to claim neutrality. (Quinn's namesake pub, adjacent to the armory site and a hiker favorite just yards from the footpath, was destroyed in a major July 2015 fire that originated on its back patio.)

Brown was tried for treason against the state of Virginia. He was hanged on December 2, 1859, in Charles Town, about eight miles away, with one John Wilkes Booth in the crowd of spectators. Four others were executed on December 16, and another two were hanged on March 16, 1860.

In the end, at least five of John Brown's men managed to escape, including another of Brown's sons and Osborne Anderson, who wrote about his experience. Four who escaped—perhaps along the route north now taken by the A.T.—later served with the Union army.[185] (Colonel Lewis Washington five years later went to France on a diplomatic mission for the Confederacy. His second wife, Ella, secured a pardon for him after the war as a result of her friendship with Union General George Custer; he died at Beall-Air in 1871.)

John Brown's Fort, c.1882-1886. (Historic Photo Collection, Harpers Ferry NHP)

John Brown's moral steadfastness for the Golden Rule drove his personal mission to rid the nation of slavery and propelled him in the North as a martyr for this cause. During his publicized trial and execution, he continued to champion freedom for all. He confidently proclaimed his actions as "the greatest service man can render to God" and raised the question of when Southerners would face the issue of slavery.

Idealistically, he had hoped for a peaceful revolution for universal freedom. Although Washington testified against him (while noting his good treatment), one of his prisoners, John E.P. Dangerfield, chose not to attend Brown's execution, despite having been hostage for more than 60 hours and having lived in "constant dread of being shot." He said he witnessed compassion in Brown for not taking "a life for a life" when his sons were shot.

In the face of his own death, he disposed of his hope for a peaceful liberation of slaves and proclaimed that America could not unseat the reins of slavery without bloodshed:

> *I John Brown, am quite certain that the crimes of this guilty land will never be purged away but with blood. I had, as I now think vainly, flattered myself that without very much bloodshed it might be done.*[186]

His vision foreshadowed the next stage of American history—bloodshed and inevitable war.

From 1895-1909, John Brown's Fort stood on the Alexander Murphy Farm on a bluff overlooking the Shenandoah River. (Historic Photo Collection, Harpers Ferry NHP)

The 1848 structure he had "captured" served as the engine house for the federal armory. The fort has been moved four times. It now sits beside the Appalachian Trail 150 feet from its location during the 1859 raid. Today, a marker on the railroad embankment just to the north marks the original location of the fort.

The smallest of the armory buildings, it was miraculously spared from burning in 1861 when retreating Federals destroyed the arsenal, as well as when Confederates burned much of the rest of Harpers Ferry a few months later. It remained intact during the arson of "The Point"—the strip of land adjacent to it now that overlooks the rivers' confluence—to prevent sharpshooters from finding haven there in 1862 and throughout the rest of the war.

In 1891, it was dismantled and moved to Chicago as part of the Columbia Exposition Fair. It was returned to Harpers Ferry and reassembled on nearby Murphy farm in 1895. Gradually, it fell into disrepair on the farm and was being used for grain storage when administrators of Storer College—an all-black school that was given a large part of the old armory's housing and administrative facilities on Camp Hill (see page 107) after the war—began a campaign to relocate it again. They were successful, and the building was dismantled and rebuilt on the campus in 1909, coinciding with the fiftieth anniversary of the raid. Decades later, after large parts of the town and all of Storer were acquired for the national historical park and a handful of other National Park Service functions, the agency raised and lowered it onto trucks to relocate the engine house in 1968 to its current location in the lower part of town. (See page 109.)

1861: The War Begins

Following Brown's raid in October 1859, U.S. troops were assigned to Harpers Ferry to guard the armory and arsenal. The arsenal comprised a small building and a large building surrounded by a stone wall and a tall fence.[187] The nation's leadership, uneasy with strains developing between North and South political figures, sought to protect weapons there and thwart any attack that could further compromise the stability of the Union. In the months leading up to April 1861, 90,000 arms from Harpers Ferry were shipped from Harpers Ferry to other arsenals. Fewer arms remained in Harpers Ferry than many in Virginia thought. What did remain was to be kept out of the hands of Secessionists.

In 1906, the Second Niagara Conference met in Harpers Ferry on the Storer College campus through which the blue-blazed trail from the A.T. to ATC now passes. The meeting of this precursor to the national Association for the Advancement of Colored People, led by W.E.B. Du Bois (see page 107) included a site visit to John Brown's fort, then located at the Murphy farm a short distance south of Harpers Ferry proper. Some in the procession took off their shoes to walk more closely to this hallowed ground.

On April 12, 1861, the War Between the States began with shots fired at the U.S. garrison on Fort Sumter, off the sea battery of Charleston, South Carolina. Five days later, Virginia seceded, joining the seven other states that had already ratified the Confederate Constitution following South Carolina's rebellion on December 20, 1860.

On April 18, the fears of the Union's leadership were realized when three units of Virginia militia were positioned in Charles Town and approached Harpers Ferry to secure additional arms and munitions for the battles ahead.

Led by his instincts, as well as rumors of an attack, Lt. Roger Jones, who was in charge of protecting the arsenal, devised a plan to defend or destroy it before it fell into Secessionists' hands. He packed the buildings with one hundred pounds of gun powder, added straw and wood chips to the mound of flammables, and awaited the imminent arrival of Virginians.[188] When Jones received word of the approaching militia at 10 p.m., he swiftly ignited the two arsenal buildings, causing a large explosion and the elimination of 15,000 arms,[189] and then retreated over the Potomac River into Maryland.

The two arsenal buildings and the carpenter shop were thoroughly destroyed, and a stock-turning shop and storehouse also were burned. Townspeople and members of the Virginia militia worked together to put out the fires before they spread to the rest of town. In three months' time, it would be Secessionists who set fire to Harpers Ferry before leaving.

Harpers Ferry, occupied by Secessionists after Jones' retreat, was ravaged for supplies to support the Southern cause. They rounded up tools and fabrication machinery from the armory and the rifle factory on Virginius Island, as well as parts for unfinished muskets, and sent all of it south on trains bound for Richmond, Virginia, and Fayetteville, North Carolina.[190] With those resources, the Confederacy could make as many arms as they lost in failing to capture the arsenal and more.[191]

The Confederates held Harpers Ferry in this initial stage of the war from April 18 to June 15, 1861.[192] In this period, they built blockhouses on Loudoun Heights and fortifications on Maryland Heights.[193] (See pages 77 and 105.) Colonel Thomas "Stonewall" Jackson commanded 8,000 troops in Harpers Ferry[194] until his command was transferred to General Joseph Johnston in mid-May.[195] Within three weeks of his command of Harpers Ferry, Johnston determined that it was indefensible and began the process of dismantling the Confederate military installation. Supplies useful to the cause that had not already been sent south were gathered and sent to Richmond. Then, according to the account of one Georgia soldier, "All the fortifications were also destroyed, except two on the east side of the Shenandoah [Loudoun Heights], which still command the Ferry, and are as impregnable as the rocks of Gibraltar."[196]

The retreating Confederates burned public buildings in town and the bridge over the Potomac on June 14[197] and returned on June 28 to burn the rifle factory and a covered bridge over the Shenandoah River.[198]

Harpers Ferry was isolated and abandoned, but only briefly. Federal troops returned again for part of July and August but did not formally occupy the town again until 1862. The succession of control from U.S. to Confederate troops in April, the abandonment of the post by Confederates in June, and the subsequent control by Federals constitute the first three of the eight times the town changed hands during the war.

> Adjacent to Harpers Ferry to the west, the Battle of Bolivar Heights occurred on October 16, 1861. In a clash between roughly equal numbers, the Union fought off the Confederates who retreated to the Shenandoah Valley.

Union soldiers on Camp Hill in 1862. A Union camp is visible on Bolivar Heights in the distance. (Historic Photo Collection, Harpers Ferry NHP)

1862: The Siege of Harpers Ferry

Union troops officially returned to Harpers Ferry in February 1862. Their purpose was to rebuild bridges and railroads then oversee the continued protection of railroad supply and communications lines.

That spring, Stonewall Jackson moved swiftly through the Shenandoah Valley and secured Confederate victories in Front Royal and Winchester, cities that now are connected by I-81 through the valley. Confederate forces continued north and east to threaten Washington, D.C. In response, Federals set up a battery of naval guns on the Maryland slope overlooking Harpers Ferry.[199]

June through early September were relatively quiet months for the troops stationed in Harpers Ferry. But in early September, Confederates captured Harpers Ferry, took 12,500 Federal troops prisoner, seized between 11,000 and 13,000 small arms, and captured 73 cannons.[200]

That siege began as now-Confederate General Robert E. Lee invaded Maryland on September 4, 1862, planning to destroy a railroad bridge over the Susquehanna River at Harrisburg, Pennsylvania. His strategy included cutting off an attack from behind by eliminating the danger posed by Union troops in Harpers Ferry. By gaining control of the town, Lee also would ensure the disruption of Federal communications and movements of troops and equipment. He might also garner some needed stores for his haggard troops.

"Stonewall" Jackson reviews captured Federal prisoners on Bolivar Heights on September 15, 1862. (Commissioned Art Collection, Harpers Ferry Center, National Park Service)

Lee sent Generals Jackson, John G. Walker, and Lafayette McLaws to secure Harpers Ferry in a coordinated attack from the west near Bolivar Heights, the east at Loudoun Heights, and the north from Maryland Heights, respectively. Lee issued the orders on September 9. By 10 a.m. on September 13, Walker and his command were in place with five rifled cannons on Loudoun Heights. Maryland Heights had been moderately defended until the afternoon of the 13th when it was suddenly relinquished to the invading Confederates[201] under McLaws. Jackson was in Martinsburg (about fifteen miles northwest) on the 14th; he forced the Union troops he found there to retreat toward Harpers Ferry. He followed.[202] The combined Federal forces were completely surrounded by Jackson's troops on Schoolhouse Ridge to the west and A.P. Hill's troops coming up Bolivar Heights from the south. All that was left for them to do was surrender. (See page 78.) Lacking the resources to hold them and eager to move north, Jackson ordered the Union troops to be paroled.

The Union defeat in Harpers Ferry on September 15 was the largest surrender of U.S. forces during the Civil War and the largest capitulation of U.S. military until the fall of Bataan to the Japanese in the Philippines during World War II.

As Harpers Ferry fell to Jackson, a bloody battle was raging due north on South Mountain in Maryland. Confederates were sorely outnumbered but fought courageously, losing a lot of soldiers but maintaining the gaps until nightfall, when fighting ceased and they retreated from the crest. (The A.T. now bisects this battlefield. See page 115.)

Following the fall of Harpers Ferry, Generals Walker, Jackson, and McLaws headed to Maryland as promptly as possible to reinforce the dwindling Confederates on South Mountain. The reunion of the Confederate armies outside the town of Sharpsburg along Antietam Creek and the arrival of Union forces in the next few days ended in the single bloodiest day of battle of the entire Civil War—the Battle of Antietam/Sharpsburg on September 17, 1862.

By September 18, Confederates had left Harpers Ferry altogether,[203] but it was only two days later that the Union returned there from Sharpsburg. Following their demoralizing defeat at Harpers Ferry less than a week earlier, Federals took seriously the defense of the town offered by the heights. They increased fortifications on Loudoun Heights by building stone redoubts, installing a road and a signal station. On Maryland Heights, they dug powder magazines and built a thirty-pound artillery battery.[204]

1863: A Quieter Year

Federals retained a stronghold on Harpers Ferry and continued to reinforce their defensive position by adding a stone fort, a hundred-pound cannon, and another thirty-pound battery on Maryland Heights.

General Lee made a second foray into northern territory that culminated in the Battle of Gettysburg on July 1-3, 1863. Just prior to and following Gettysburg, a couple skirmishes occurred around Harpers Ferry: One on June 30, when Virginia cavalry attacked a Union camp on Bolivar Heights and captured 20 soldiers and as many horses; the second on July 14, also near Bolivar Heights.[205]

1864: Suddenly Awakened and on Edge

The Maryland cavalry on Loudoun Heights were abruptly awoken in the wee hours of January 10, 1864, by a sneak attack from Colonel John S. Mosby and his band of Partisan Rangers. Thus began a year of intense harassment by Mosby of the Union troops stationed in Harpers Ferry and the surrounding area. As a result, the Federal garrison assigned to protect the Baltimore & Ohio Railroad and the C&O Canal was increased to 8,000.[206]

On June 28, Union forces from Harpers Ferry chased Mosby's men from Charles Town as another group of rangers raided stores of Duffields Depot west of Harpers Ferry, even today a railroad passenger stop, and cut communications lines between Harpers Ferry and the larger town of Martinsburg to the west.[207]

Following General David Hunter's raid, the Battle of Lynchburg, and the subsequent retreat of Union forces into West Virginia (see page 49), Confederate General Jubal

A. Early took the opportunity to head north into Maryland again. Early's raid on Washington began with a northward sweep down the Shenandoah Valley. Some of his forces pushed toward Harpers Ferry on July 4 and induced the retreat of Federal forces to Maryland Heights to defend the town. Firing from the heights is said to have prevented Confederate forces from fording the Potomac and reaching Maryland.[208] Other historians suspect that the small force that moved into Harpers Ferry was a feint to throw the Union off from Early's actual destination.[209] In any case, the abandonment of the town by Federal forces and the Confederate occupation, however brief, signaled the sixth and seventh times the town changed hands.

In early August, General Philip H. Sheridan was given command of the Union forces and ordered troops to control and destroy any provisions available in the Shenandoah Valley—a main artery to the heart of the Confederacy. His command headquarters were in Harpers Ferry, and from there he led troops south up the valley to strip it bare.

Partisan Rangers of the 43rd Virginia continued to peck away at the communications and supply lines of the Federals. They attacked wagon trains if they were inadequately guarded, as they did on August 12 in the Berryville Wagon Raid (see page 71). The tactics of the rangers required additional Federal military personnel to escort the wagon trains, distracting them from other fronts.

On October 14, Mosby's men derailed a train on the Baltimore & Ohio line not far from Harp-

Philip H. Sheridan. (Library of Congress)

ers Ferry. The raid on this passenger train wasn't a large military boost for the Confederates, rather an annoyance to the Federal installation in the area charged with protecting the rail lines. Two Union paymasters on board were discovered with up to $173,000 of "greenbacks" in pay for on-duty soldiers. The rangers absconded with the money and burned the train; that was the extent of the victory. The Union repaired the railroad line within a few days. (See page 72.)

As 1864 rolled in to 1865, fighting continued in the Shenandoah Valley and other parts of Virginia, Alabama, Georgia, Tennessee, but relatively limited activity occurred in Harpers Ferry in the final months leading up to Lee's surrender.

Camp Hill and Appalachian Trail Discovery Amble

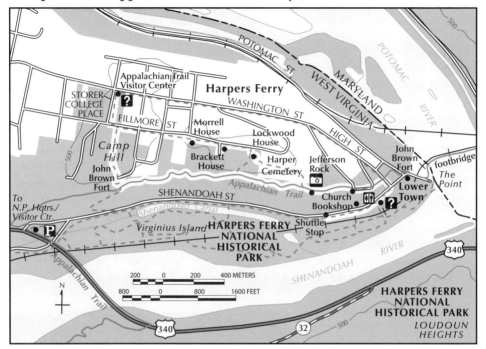

Distance: 1.9 mile

Difficulty: Moderate

Trailhead directions: For this hike, recommended parking is at the main Harpers Ferry National Historical Park entrance on the southern side of U.S. 340 at the top of the hill southwest of town, since parking on Camp Hill is limited to residents, short-term ATC visitors, and park staff. The park offers shuttle service directly to the lower town where this hike begins. It costs $6 per vehicle for three consecutive days, beginning on the day of purchase. With this in mind, hikers might plan to hike Loudoun Heights one day and Maryland Heights one day and spend another day exploring Harpers Ferry near the A.T.

Description: From the shuttle stop in the lower town, walk east along Shenandoah Street toward the Potomac. Pass the bookstore and public restrooms on your left. Turn left on High Street, pass a building housing a Black Voices museum, and ascend the stone steps cut from the bedrock; you are now on the Appalachian Trail. The peculiar, uneven, and steep staircase is an excellent example of the historical perspective offered throughout the town. Walk then along a paved section of road for a short distance to pass St. Peter's Roman Catholic Church. The white blazes lead up another set of stairs. As you climb those stairs, the remains of St. John's Episcopal Church are on your right; the church served as a barracks and hospital during the war.

    The footpath returns to dirt and soon leads to Jefferson Rock. Take the opportunity to enjoy "one of the most stupendous scenes in Nature," as Jefferson described it.[210] To switch your historical mindset a century or so, consider that the finishing touches on the retaining wall next to Jefferson Rock were put on in April 1998 by then-President Bill Clinton and Vice President Al Gore during an Earth Day visit to the A.T., "the people's path," as Clinton dubbed it.

Once you resume your hike on the A.T., you will reach a stone-steps junction on the right for Harper Cemetery placed by a special ATC crew in the late 1990s. Follow a winding path of your choice through the historical grounds but eventually walk westward toward the Lockwood House, named for the Union general (Henry H.) who used the house as his headquarters during the war. It was later the very first building deeded to Storer College and now serves as office space for park interpeters.

Walk west for four blocks along Fillmore Street. On your left, you will pass the Brackett House and the Morrell House, both used once by Storer College and now by the park's administration. (Brackett House also was the headquarters of the then Appalachian Trail Conference from 1971 to 1976.) Continuing until you reach Storer College Place, you will walk through a residential neighborhood. At Storer College Place, turn right and walk one block to the Appalachian Trail Conservancy (ATC) headquarters and visitors center that offers advice to hikers and information about the Trail. The conservancy is often a milestone in the pilgrimages of travelers of this long-distance trail; Harpers Ferry is viewed as the psychological halfway point of the more than 2,189 miles of the Appalachian Trail.

Retrace Storer College Place back to Fillmore Street to the sidewalk on the other side of Fillmore. You have been on Camp Hill for a few blocks and now are basically on its summit. Passing through the wrought-iron gateway and heading south on a blue-blazed A.T. side trail, you are approaching Wirth Hall (known as Anthony Hall in Storer College days and the armorer's residence in antebellum days) and the Mather Training Center on your right. Now used by the National Park Service, this building was used during the Civil War as a headquarters for the Second Corps of the Army of the Potomac.[211] During the war, President Lincoln spent at least one night upstairs. Decades after the war, it was also the site of the Second Niagara Movement meeting (see page 107).

The building is captured in famous photographs of Camp Hill with tents and soldiers in formation. Look up to the east and you will understand how troops on Loudoun Heights (right) and Maryland Heights (left) could so

National Park Service wayfinding sign for the Appalachian Trail in Harpers Ferry. (Photo by David T. Gilbert)

easily bombard the town and encampments, especially with most of the trees removed.

Pass the stone building on your left at the end of the walkway that once served held classrooms and laboratories for Storer College and now houses the offices of the Appalachian National Scenic Trail (NPS' oversight agency for the A.T.). Directly ahead of you is the 1909–1968 site of John Brown's "Fort." A tablet commemorating John Brown's raid that had been commissioned in 1932 by famous author and civil-rights activist William Edward Burghardt (W.E.B.) Du Bois (born in Great Barrington, Massachusetts, just steps

Wirth Hall on Camp Hill now houses the National Park Service Stephen T. Mather Training Center. (Photo by David T. Gilbert)

away from the future route of the A.T.) was dedicated at this site on July 14, 2006. (See pages 111-113.)

Follow the blue blazes and signs indicating a side trail to the Appalachian Trail that leads between the stone building and the former site of the engine house. Descend steps, and follow the path 0.1 mile to a junction with the Appalachian Trail. Turn left at the junction to return to the lower town past Jefferson Rock and the churches and down the stone steps.

Other Activities: Either on your return from this amble or before setting out on the stone steps, plan to visit the exhibits on Storer College and the Niagara Movement in the building on the corner of High and Shenandoah streets.

Once you have visited the imagined original and current sites of John Brown's "fort" in the lower town, as well as the site when it was on the Storer College campus, consider walking the 2.2 miles to Murphy Farm to cover the range of local movement of this structure. Another nearby hike rich with Civil War history is a 0.75-mile hike at Bolivar Heights. Maps for all these hikes and other adventures in Harpers Ferry are available at the ATC visitors center.

Virginius Island and Lower Town Loop

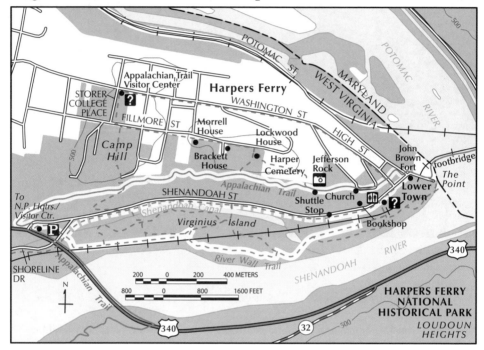

Distance: 1.8 mile

Difficulty: Easy

Trailhead directions: Park at the lot near the intersection of Shenandoah Street and U.S. 340 or, if parking is not available there, at the main Harpers Ferry National Historical Park entrance up the hill on the southern side of the highway. Parking at either location costs $6 per vehicle, and the fee covers three consecutive days, beginning on the day of purchase. In the latter case, take the shuttle to the lower town to begin this hike. If you park in the lot on Shenandoah Street, walk up the street toward town until you reach the shuttle stop on the right by a bus parking lot.

Description: This hike begins at the shuttle stop in the lower town. Walk east along Shenandoah Street. Pass the bookstore and public restrooms on your left.

As you pass High Street on your left, you will see the foundation of buildings on your right. This was the site of arsenal square that was burned April 18, 1861, by retreating Federals. Explore John Brown's Fort that sits beyond the arsenal remains where the Appalachian Trail comes out of Potomac Street to cross Shenandoah and head toward the bridge into Maryland. Park guides are often here to interpret the fort and answer questions about the history of the area. The John Brown exhibit is located just across Shenandoah Street; stop in now or on your return from The Point later in the hike. It is extremely helpful to have an accurate visual sense of this area as it was at the beginning of the war.

From here, connect John Brown's fort to the site of its original location by tracing the path with your footprints. Walk across Shenandoah Street on a diagonal toward Potomac Street. Your destination is the top of the railroad embankment. Walk up the steps to an

This 1857 lithograph shows the industrial village of Virginius Island on the banks of the Shenandoah River. Today virtually nothing remains of this once thriving community. (Historic Photo Collection, Harpers Ferry NHP)

obelisk that marks the site of the old engine house.

After contemplating John Brown's defensive position in the fort, descend the steps, and pass under the railroad bridge toward "The Point." Visitors today are greeted by the aesthetic of the land carved by rivers: the cliffs of Maryland and Loudoun heights on either side of the town. They have to imagine what it looked like leading up to February 1862 when the area was burned to thwart Confederate sharpshooters. Before it was burned, the Point was dense with buildings, including a saloon, jewelry store, barber shop, and clothing stores. Since in 1859 and throughout the war the slopes of the heights were cleared of trees, visitors can imagine the way that military installations on the crests could easily see from one heights' signal station to another, observe the town, and rain down cannonballs.

The supports of the bridge that formerly spanned the Potomac River are still visible. That was the bridge crossed by John Brown; it was destroyed and rebuilt nine times during the war.[212]

Take leave of the Point by heading back to Shenandoah Street. (The next portion of this hike coincides with the Camp Hill Appalachian Trail Amble Hike. You can skip that by strolling away from town along Shenandoah Street and walking the "goat trail" on the eastbound shoulder of Shenandoah Street. It's a pleasant walk alongside an old canal and offers the opportunity to stop by the ruins of the pulp mill, which this hike does not otherwise pass.)

If you want to stick to the Appalachian Trail, cross Shenandoah onto Potomac Street, turn left at the first break in the buildings, and walk along their "backyards" to High Street, then cross it to the stone steps, and ascend them. Walk along a paved section of road for a short distance to pass by St. Peter's Roman Catholic Church. The white blazes lead up another set of stairs. As you climb those stairs, the remains of St. John's Episcopal Church are on your right; the church served as a barracks and hospital during the war.

The footpath returns to dirt and soon leads to Jefferson Rock. After Jefferson Rock, the Trail undulates gently along the ridge for almost a mile, passing steps up to Harper Cemetery and later a side trail for the Appalachian Trail Conservancy office and visitors center. The trail drops gradually to meet U.S. 340. Staying on the northern side of the highway, cross Shenandoah Street, and take the sidewalk down to the parking lot on your right.

Cross through the parking lot to the southeast corner near a kiosk. For hikers who opted for the trail along the shoulder of Shenandoah Street, pick up the hike here.

Ascend the short staircase, and watch for traffic as you cross Shoreline Drive. Here the path is wide and approaches the railroad tracks. Before reaching the tracks, turn left on a footpath to parallel the tracks. Walk 0.22 mile to a four-way intersection of trails. Follow the one on your right to cross over the railroad tracks and follow the River Wall Trail. Along this path, pass the ruins of water tunnels, the cotton mill, blacksmith shop, machine shops, and plenty of interpretive signs about the industry and history of Virginius Island. The interloping trails of Virginius Island should be explored; if you have the time, you may opt to veer off this planned hike to follow the paths and gain a deeper understanding of the island, once a "little Pittsburgh" along the Shenandoah.

If you plan to stay the course for the remainder of this hike, or if you have resumed it where you left off to explore, follow the River Wall Trail on a wood-planked bridge over the Shenandoah Canal. In the summer, the shoreline park setting on your right offers the opportunity to bask on the grass or dip your toes in the cool river waters. (Swimming is prohibited.) The shuttle stop is just ahead on the left on the other side of the trestle.

Other Activities: Notable exhibits in Harpers Ferry National Historical Park are the Black Voices, Civil War, Storer College, and Niagara Conference offerings on High Street and the John Brown exhibit on Shenandoah Street.

Since this hike offers a close-up look at Harpers Ferry circa 1859, visitors with a keen interest in John Brown may opt to take a short drive into Maryland to Kennedy Farm, now a state historical site. The farmhouse is fenced off and viewable from a distance unless you call in advance to arrange a visit. Call (301) 652-2857 or (301) 977-3599 for a tour.

Maryland Heights Hike

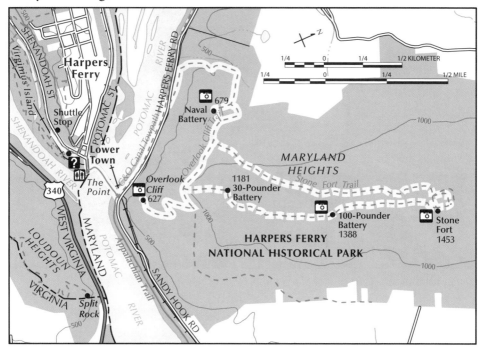

Distance: 4.5 or 6.5 miles

Difficulty: Strenuous

Trailhead directions: Park at Harpers Ferry National Historical Park main entrance on U.S. 340 and take the shuttle to the lower town.

Description: While only the first 0.3 or 0.4 mile of this hike is on the Appalachian Trail, its rich history, commanding view of Harpers Ferry, and ranking as a favorite hike in this area are reasons enough to spend a day exploring Maryland Heights. Walk along Shenandoah Street to John Brown's "Fort." Turn right on the A.T. to pass under a railroad overpass and toward the Point. Follow directional signs to the cantilevered pedestrian walkway on the railroad bridge over the Potomac River. Descend the stairs, and turn left on the hard-packed sandy towpath of the C&O Canal. You've tracked 0.3 mile of the hike so far. Follow the canal for a half-mile. Look for and take a wooden bridge over the canal ditch on your right. Cross over Harpers Ferry Road to a wide pull-off and the approach to the trail. A kiosk about the trails of Maryland Heights confirms that you are on the right track. Follow the green blazes up the steep trail for 0.7 mile. Breathless, you'll reach another kiosk that describes the military road to your left. Consider the steep terrain of the road, but take the junction on the right toward the cliffs. You are now following red blazing on trees. In 0.2 mile, reach a junction on the left with a blue-blazed trail to the Stone Fort; pass it by this time. Walk 0.4 mile to the rewarding overlook of the cliffs. On a clear day, it's almost impossible to take a bad picture of the sweet hamlet of Harpers Ferry from here. After you have enjoyed the views from the cliffs, you can return to Harpers Ferry the way you came, or continue on to the Stone Fort, the batteries, and the summit of Maryland Heights.

Stone Fort ruins along the crest of Maryland Heights. (Photo by David T. Gilbert)

If you decide to carry on for the longer hike, congratulations are in order because the hardest part of this hike is behind you. Trace your steps back 0.4 mile to the junction with the blue-blazed Stone Fort Trail. Take the junction on your right. While the trail is steep in this section, the frequency of historic sites allows for rewarding rest stops.

Standing at the site of the hundred-pound Dahlgren gun is breathtaking. (A Parrott gun with the same capacity replaced it in 1863.) Not only is the view super, but it gives perspective to the grit and determination of the men and horses or mules required to haul the 9,700-pound cannon up to the height of the ridge.

Follow the blue blazes to reach the massive structure of the Stone Fort. Interpretive signs in the area explain the space and design of the building. Descend several steps, and pass through a relatively flat area once used as a camp.

The trail now connects with the military road you had gazed at earlier, thinking, "My goodness, *that* is steep!" Watch your step on this rocky descent. Follow the steep military road for 0.9 mile to its intersection with the green-blazed Combined Trail. Turn right to retrace your steps, and return to lower Harpers Ferry where you began.

Harpers Ferry after the War

Storer College

The year the Civil War ended and three years after the Emancipation Proclamation was issued, a primary school was established in Harpers Ferry to provide an education to former slaves. Some people closest to the development of the school, members of the Freewill Baptist Church, questioned the likelihood of its success, likening it to "a railroad to the moon."[213] Students and teachers were discouraged by angry and often violent encounters with local community members,[214] but the school and its student enrollment grew.

The primary school that started in one building, the Lockwood House, grew to 2,500 students by 1867.[215] In October of that year, the school's founder, the Rev. Dr. Nathan Cook Brackett, received funding from philanthropist John Storer of Maine. The $10,000 gift from Storer required that the school be open to anyone, regardless of gender, race, or religious belief, and the institution became known as the Storer Normal School. The funds and the formal transfer of the Lockwood House and three other former armory buildings from the federal government to the school in 1869 allowed the school to offer greater educational opportunities to even more students.[216]

The Storer campus on Camp Hill in Harpers Ferry was chartered by the state of West Virginia in 1869, and the first class graduated in 1872. These graduates were trained so that they could teach students at other freedmen schools.[217] Storer College was among the first institutions in the post-war United States to educate African-Americans. Its board of trustees included reformer and orator Frederick Douglass, who gave a speech at the college in May 1881 in which he extolled John Brown's virtues, sacrifices, and contributions to the advancement of blacks as free citizens of the nation.[218]

The rich history of Brown's deeds in Harpers Ferry brought the Niagara Movement, a precursor to the National Association for the Advancement of Colored People, to Harpers Ferry for a conference in 1906 at Storer College (see below).

The college lost funding from federal and state sources following the desegregation of schools with the 1954 *Brown v. Board of Education* Supreme Court decision, and it closed in 1955.[219]

Niagara Movement

The legacy of John Brown's struggle for human equality brought the Niagara Movement to Harpers Ferry in 1906 for its second conference. Held August 15-19, the program featured speakers, assessments of civic and political situations,

Niagara Conference attendees pose in front of Anthony Hall—now known as Wirth Hall—at the conclusion of the 1906 Niagara Conference on the campus of Storer College in Harpers Ferry. The building is on the A.T. side trail. (Historic Photo Collection, Harpers Ferry NHP)

and discussions on reforms related to crime, health, education, and the media.[220] Nearly 100 attendees convened at the Storer College campus.[221] They walked from the campus to the Murphy Farm, where John Brown's "fort" had been located since 1894, in a "silent procession" to honor the sacrifice Brown made in the name of liberty of all.[222]

At the conclusion of the conference, W.E.B. Du Bois read a resolution that summed up the desires of the movement's constituents and served as a message to the nation on social inequalities:

> *In detail, our demands are clear and unequivocal. First, we would vote; with the right to vote goes everything, freedom, manhood, the honor of our wives, the chastity of our daughters, the right to work, and the chance to rise and let no man listen to those who deny this.*
>
> *We want full manhood suffrage and we want it now, henceforth and forever.*
>
> *Second. We want discrimination in public accommodation to cease. Separation in railway and street cars, based simply on race and color, is un-American, undemocratic and silly. We protest against all such discrimination.*

Third. We claim the right of freemen to walk, talk and be with who wish to be with us. No man has a right to choose another man's friends and to attempt to do so is an impudent interference with the most fundamental human privilege.

Fourth. We want the law enforced against rich as well as poor, against Capitalist as well as Laborer; against white as well as black. We are not more lawless than the white race; we are more often arrested, convicted and mobbed. We want justice even for criminals and outlaws. We want the Constitution of the country enforced. We want Congress to take charge of the Congressional elections. We want the Fourteenth Amendment carried out to the letter and every State disenfranchised in Congress which attempts to disenfranchise its rightful voters. We want the Fifteenth Amendment enforced and no State allowed to have its franchise on color.

Fifth. We want our children educated. The school system in the country districts of the South is a disgrace and in few towns and cities are the Negro schools what they ought to be. We want the national government to step in and wipe out illiteracy in the South. Either the United States will destroy ignorance or ignorance will destroy the United States.[223]

The first meeting of the Niagara Movement had been along the Niagara River in Ontario and hosted twenty-nine men from fourteen states. Its members met again in 1907, 1908, and 1909 in Massachusetts, Ohio, and New Jersey, respectively, but by 1911 the organization had been dissolved. Niagara Movement founder Du Bois urged its members to join the NAACP to continue to advocate for civil rights.[224]

John Brown's "Fort"

Miraculously, John Brown's "fort" was not burned, destroyed by cannon fire, or otherwise demolished during the years of fighting in Harpers Ferry over the course of the war. Left intact, it was a relic of Brown's failed 1859 mission that has, throughout history, served as a spectacle, a symbol of sacrifice, and a centerpiece of power. Indeed, for some time after the war, "John Brown's Fort" was painted above its doors, and it served as a tourist attraction in the otherwise rundown town.

David Gilbert writes on the Harpers Ferry National Historical Park Web site of the curious relocations of the structure this way:

In 1891, the fort was sold, dismantled, and transported to Chicago, where it was displayed a short distance from The World's Columbian Exposition. The building, attracting only 11 visitors in ten days, was closed, dismantled again, and left on a vacant lot.

In 1894, Washington, D.C., journalist Kate Field, who had a keen interest in preserving memorabilia of John Brown, spearheaded a campaign to return the fort to Harpers Ferry. Local resident Alexander Murphy made five acres available to Miss Field, and the Baltimore & Ohio Railroad offered to ship the disassembled fort to Harpers Ferry free of charge. In 1895, John Brown's Fort was rebuilt on the Murphy Farm about three miles outside of town on a bluff overlooking the Shenandoah River.

In 1903, Storer College began its own fund-raising drive to acquire the structure. In 1909, on the occasion of the 50th anniversary of John Brown's raid, the building was purchased and moved to the Storer College campus on Camp Hill in Harpers Ferry.

Acquired by the National Park Service in 1960, the building was moved back to the Lower Town in 1968. Because the fort's original site was covered with a railroad embankment in 1894, the building now sits about 150 feet east of its original location.[225]

Should funds ever become available to dig out the embankments that cover the old armory sites, the park hopes to relocate the engine house to its original location one day.[226]

A stone oblisk marks the fill above the original location of John Brown's Fort. (Photo by David T. Gilbert)

William Edward Burghardt Du Bois has a dual connection to places on or near the Appalachian Trail—Harpers Ferry in West Virginia and Great Barrington in Massachusetts.

Most significantly, W.E.B. Du Bois was a "principal architect in the civil rights movement of the United States,"[227] and he brought the founding organization for civil rights, the Niagara Movement, to Harpers Ferry in 1906 for its second conference when he was 38 years old. The Niagara Movement was the organization that preceded the National Association for the Advancement of Colored People (NAACP) in its work for equal rights.

Niagara Movement members at Harpers Ferry in 1906. W.E.B. Du Bois is seated in front. (Historic Photo Collection, Harpers Ferry NHP)

As a scholar, Du Bois wrote sixteen books, including one published in 1909 on John Brown's 1859 raid on Harpers Ferry and others particularly related to race relations and sociology. He was the first African-American to earn a doctorate from Harvard, and he taught at schools and universities in Georgia, Ohio, Pennsylvania, and New York.

Du Bois was born in February 1868 in Great Barrington, Massachusetts, roughly four miles from the current Appalachian Trail, which meanders above the eastern shore of the Housatonic River there. His parents had rented a small rear dwelling on Church Street owned by a former South Carolina slave. He described his hometown this way:

> *I was born by a golden river and in the shadow of two great hills. My birthplace was Great Barrington, a little town in western Massachusetts in the valley of the Housatonic, flanked by the Berkshire Hills.[228]*

He was raised in different houses in Great Barrington. One was on Church Street, one was above the stables on the Increase Sumner estate, and another was his grandfather Othello Burghardt's homestead on current Mass. 42/23. Neither of the homes remain, although plaques dedicated to his birthplace and his childhood home can be seen at or near both.[229]

Du Bois Point-to-Point Hike, Great Barrington, Massachusetts

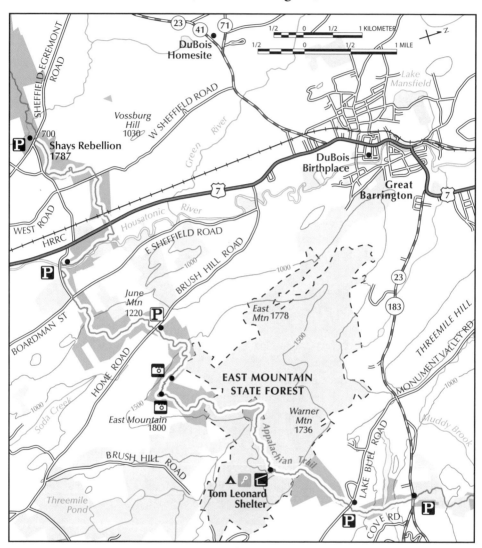

Distance: 10.2 miles

Difficulty: Moderately difficult

Directions: Since this is a point-to-point hike, hikers will be required to leave their vehicle at their destination and take a shuttle (www.appalachiantrail.org/shuttle) to the beginning of the hike or utilize two cars, one at either end of the hike. Leave a vehicle at the twelve-space parking area on Mass. 23 east of Great Barrington, and take the shuttle to Sheffield Road, also called Sheffield-Egremont Road at the spot you want.

Description: The hike begins near the site of the end of Daniel Shays Rebellion in 1787. Visit the battle-site monument before setting out on the Trail, north toward U.S. 7 and the

Stone monument on the grounds of the W.E.B. Du Bois Boyhood Homesite in Great Barrington, Mass. (ATC Photo)

Housatonic River. The first 3.5 miles of walking on the white-blazed Appalachian Trail are along the relatively flat terrain of the wide Housatonic River valley. The sounds of the river and the easy walking are a treat before you set out to tackle a 1,000-foot elevation gain.

Take the ridge of East Mountain for the next 2.4 miles. From the crest, vistas point north toward Great Barrington and south toward Sheffield. With the most significant climb of the hike now behind you, the A.T. gradually loses elevation but remains high on the ridge to reach Ice Gulch and Tom Leonard Shelter in 2.1 miles. The last two miles of the hike descend 500 feet to conclude your hike at your vehicle at Mass. 23.

Other Activities: That hike enjoys the terrain of the wide Housatonic River Valley and sweeps around the birthplace and childhood home of W.E.B. Du Bois. Hikers can easily visit both sites from trailheads at either end of this hike or by parking in town and availing oneself of a local walking-tour map.

From the Appalachian Trail crossing of Sheffield-Egremont Road, it is 3.5 miles west (north) to the Friends of Du Bois Homesite. Trail visitors may chose to continue into Great Barrington to visit his birthplace and walk along the nearby Great Barrington River-walk, or return to the A.T. to hike northbound.

From the Appalachian Trail crossing of Mass. 23, just north of Lake Buel Road, it is four miles to downtown Great Barrington and Du Bois' birthplace on Church Street. Visitors interested in W.E.B Du Bois history as well as other African-American heritage sites in the area can find information on both as part of driving and walking tours by visiting *www.Du BoisHomesite.org* and *www.AfricanAmericanTrails.org*.

More information about the trail in Harpers Ferry, along with more history of nearby points, can be found in the *Appalachian Trail Guide to Maryland–Northern Virginia* and *A Walker's Guide to Harpers Ferry,* available at the Ultimate Appalachian Trail Store° (*www.atctrailstore.org*). The Great Barrington area is covered in the *Appalachian Trail Guide to Massachusetts–Connecticut.*

View from Annapolis Rock along the Appalachian Trail in Maryland. (© Can Stock Photo)

The Maryland Campaign

The South had won significant battles in the early years of the war in campaigns in the Shenandoah Valley and in northern Virginia, despite being outnumbered.[230] Throughout the summer of 1862, the battles in the East had given Southerners confidence that the end of the war was near.

Noted historian and author James M. McPherson, in *Crossroads of Freedom: Antietam/Sharpsburg,* details the circumstances leading up to Confederate General Robert E. Lee's decision to enter Maryland and the potentials offered by the outcome. He breaks the potential outcomes down in this way: "Victory or defeat; foreign intervention; Lincoln's emancipation proclamation; Northern elections; the very willingness of the Northern people to keep fighting for the Union."[231]

Expanded, the rationale McPherson presents is that, by mid-1862, public support for the war in the North wavered. This posed the potential for the election of Democrats in favor of peace. That would signal Union concessions to the South and a swift conclusion to the war.[232] Great Britain and France, pinched by limited cotton exports from the South, were wary of a continued battle among the states and prepared to recommend a mediated split and acknowledge the sovereignty of the Confederacy.[233] Meanwhile, Lincoln was poised to unfurl the Emancipation Proclamation on the presumed uptake in public support brought by the next Union victory.[234]

Ultimately, Lee sought victory, by any means. He marched his weakened, hungry, and tattered Rebel forces into Maryland on September 4, 1862.[235] He hoped the foray into Maryland would revive the Army of Northern Virginia enough to propel it into Pennsylvania to strike the railroad bridge over the Susquehanna River in Harrisburg.[236] By crippling the railroad in Harrisburg, the Baltimore & Ohio line in Harpers Ferry, and the C&O Canal,[237] he would break the supply lines of the Federals. In concert with a swift blow on other battlefronts, that might bring complete and final victory.

Lee entered the state with roughly 50,000 men.[238] He intended to revive his famished army by taking advantage of the agricultural abundance of Maryland farms. He also hoped to gain strength in numbers by giving Maryland, a slave state, the chance to rise up against its oppressor. In an address to the people of Frederick, he said, "The people of the South have long wished to aid you in throwing off this

September 1862 sketch by Alfred R. Waud showing troops marching through Middletown, Maryland, toward South Mountain. (Library of Congress)

foreign yoke, to enable you again to enjoy the inalienable rights of freedom, and restore the independence and sovereignty of your state."[239]

Lee found less sentiment toward the Southern cause than he expected. His appeal fell largely on the silent protest of shuttered doors and windows.[240]

On September 9, encamped outside Frederick, Lee orchestrated his next move— to secure Harpers Ferry. Offensively, securing Harpers Ferry would provide captured supplies to the Rebels as well as safeguard their own lines of supply and communication.[241] Defensively, Lee's plan would eliminate reinforcements for Federal forces arriving from the west on the Baltimore & Ohio rail line and allow for a reasonable line of retreat, if needed.[242]

To that end, he issued Special Orders No. 191. The plan required splitting his army over a distance of 25 miles between Harpers Ferry and Hagerstown, Maryland.[243] The portion sent to capture Harpers Ferry with General Stonewall Jackson included commands under John G. Walker and Lafayette McLaws, who were responsible for securing Loudoun and Maryland heights, respectively. Meanwhile, the remainder of Lee's army would await the return of the divided army in Hagerstown. Once the orders were issued, the armies moved swiftly to execute them. Once the Confederate armies were reunited, they would proceed to Pennsylvania.

In a fateful turn of events, a copy of Lee's orders that detailed the division of his forces was serendipitously discovered by resting Union soldiers on the morning of September 13—probably an extra set intended for one of Jackson's subordinate generals.[244] The 27th Indiana was resting in the grass in the same field outside of Fredrick that had been used several days earlier by Confederates when Sergeant John Bloss and Corporal Barton Mitchell discovered the orders wrapped around three cigars.[245] They turned their discovery over to their leadership, and it rushed it up the chain of command. By noon, Union Commanding General George B. McClellan knew the Confederate strategy and prepared to pursue, attack, and demolish them while the armies were still divided.

The importance of that unlikely Federal advantage cannot be overstated. In fact, historian McPherson calls it "a remarkable example of the contingencies that change the course of history." He argues that, without this intelligence, McClellan would have tarried longer and may have lost a significant battle on northern soil.[246]

Even with the intelligence provided in the lost orders, however, McClellan's 88,000 troops waited sixteen hours before moving toward South Mountain, the north-south ridge that defines the narrowest part of Maryland between the Potomac and the Pennsylvania border. This ridge, now the route of the Appalachian Trail, was where Federals would first clash with Confederates in the battle for Maryland. [247]

The battle of South Mountain, Sunday, September 14, 1862. (Library of Congress)

When McClellan's troops moved on South Mountain from Frederick on September 14, the Confederate army already had assumed strong defensive positions in the gaps of the ridge. Lee had received his own intelligence about the Union discovery of the lost orders and took immediate action to delay Union advances on the divided Confederate army. Lee positioned the bulk of his available troops at Turners Gap, where the A.T. now crosses Alternate U.S. 40. Generals D.H. Hill and, later, James Longstreet were ordered to hold the gap. [248] A division of troops under McLaws' command in Crampton Gap, not quite six miles to the south, had the responsibility of protecting the remainder of his troops, who had gained control of Maryland Heights ten miles away as part of the siege of Harpers Ferry.

On September 14, McClellan's Union army arrived. They charged Turners and nearby Fox gaps in the morning with 28,000 men and Crampton Gap by early afternoon with 9,000. The 12,000 Confederates assigned to hold all the gaps fought valiantly against superior numbers. By dusk, the Federals had taken Crampton Gap, and fighting at Turners and Fox gaps ceased by nightfall. By 11 p.m., all Confederate troops had withdrawn to the valley on the western side of the ridge.

According to South Mountain State Battlefield records, 2,685 Confederate and 2,325 Union casualties were suffered in the single day of fighting.[249] On South Mountain, Confederates lost twenty-two percent of their forces; the Union, six percent. Federals had another 50,000 troops who weren't even deployed in the fighting on the 14th. Newspapers reported that the Battle of South Mountain had served to "turn back the tide of the Rebel successes."[250]

The Union victory on South Mountain[251] set the stage for the classic Battle of Antietam/Sharpsburg three days later. The battle in Sharpsburg became the bloodiest day of the entire Civil War. Viewed at the time as a Federal victory, it still was fought to a near stand-still and is now commonly considered inconclusive.[252] Yet, Confederates withdrew across the Potomac into what would soon become the Eastern Panhandle of West Virginia on September 18.[253] Lincoln would capitalize on the immediate sense of Union victory to launch the Emancipation Proclamation, on paper freeing the slaves within Secessionist territory.

The Appalachian Trail now connects the sites of "a little-known but decisive Civil War battle [that] thwarted the Southern advance."[254] The Battle of South Mountain spanned 9.1 miles of the ridge, from Brownsville Gap to Turners Gap, a distance now connected by the Appalachian Trail. Since 1931, the Appalachian Trail has been located on the crest of South Mountain,[255] although a number of small relocations were made necessary by the federal and state land-acquisition programs of the late twentieth century. The Appalachian Trail passes over Loudoun Heights on the Virginia border, through the West Virginia town of Harpers Ferry that fell to Confederates during Lee's invasion, and on across the Potomac (Maryland's

View from Antietam Battlefield looking east toward South Mountain. (Photo by David T. Gilbert)

border) up to South Mountain and northward. Hikers wishing to experience the full scope and distance of the Maryland Campaign can take advantage of all 22 trail miles—from Loudoun Heights to the Washington Monument just beyond Turners Gap—with enough time, training, and desire.

According to Paula Strain, the late archivist/author and long-time Potomac Appalachian Trail Club leader, South Mountain State Park was established in 1984 to protect the backcountry experience of the A.T.[256] Certainly, land managers also considered the incidental conservation of the Civil War battlefields. South Mountain speaks volumes about nature, the history of the Civil War, the Underground Railroad, and the potential for conservation of special places.

Brownsville Gap and Crampton Gap

The struggle at Crampton Gap on September 14 started later in the day than other fighting along South Mountain. Union General William B. Franklin's troops were in Burkittsville, Maryland, by early afternoon, just 1.2 miles from the top of the gap and less than a half-mile from Confederate troops, also on the eastern side at the base of the ridge. In anticipation of the Federals' arrival, the Rebels had taken cover behind a stone wall and positioned artillery higher on the ridge.[257]

Faced with the Rebel defense at the base of the mountain, the Federals swung to the left of Burkittsville to the right flank of the Confederates, to ascertain the strength and position of the enemy. As they approached Brownsville Gap, roughly a mile south of town, they met with resistance there, too. Checked by the defense of the gaps, Franklin pulled back from Burkittsville. It wasn't until the late afternoon that his forces made another attempt to take the gap. Their afternoon assault was met with greater success, and the Southerners began to fall back, retreating up the ridge to the gap. Confederate reinforcements had been sent to the gap, but they were not enough to hold back the abundance of men in blue.

Confederates had roughly 2,150 men engaged, compared to at least 9,000 in Franklin's VI Corps.[258] During the melee, General T. Howell Cobb's Georgia Legion fought gallantly against superior forces while other Confederates retreated west and south into the valley. The Georgians, led by their former governor and the first head of the Confederacy, lost seventy-six percent of their men to capture or casualty. The Georgia Legion's valor, among other heroic actions, is commemorated in the gap.

Blasts from howitzers positioned on the ridge rained down on Federals approaching the gap, but they pushed onward and upward.[259] After three hours of hard fighting, the Federals claimed control of the gap.[260] Despite having orders to proceed to Harpers Ferry to relieve the trapped Union garrison, Franklin did not pursue the Confederates on their retreat into the valley on the western side of the ridge.

From the gap, Franklin saw a stronghold of Confederates spanning the valley west of Brownsville Gap, with artillery on the ridges of both sides. Three of McLaws' brigades from Maryland Heights had joined the survivors of the earlier fighting at Crampton Gap.[261] Franklin perceived a force equal in size to his own and credited them with the stronger position. He decided to deliberate overnight—long enough for Harpers Ferry to completely fall into Confederate hands.

Crampton Gap and George Alfred "Gath" Townsend

Crampton Gap may be the most interpreted of the Civil War battlegrounds on South Mountain. Look for interpretive signs and historical and commemorative markers that detail Confederate General Paul J. Semmes' position at Brownsville Gap, Rebel General Wade Hampton III's and Colonel Thomas T. Munford's defense of Crampton Gap, Colonel Joseph Bartlett's leading the charge for the Union, Mell's Rifles and Troup Light Artillery (part of Georgia General Cobb's infantry), the Confederate last stand, the task of burial, medals of honor bestowed on South Mountain soldiers, and the First New Jersey Brigade. An overview of the entire Maryland Campaign and the story of Lee's lost orders are located at this gap, as well as at Turners and Fox gaps.

Twenty years after the war, Crampton Gap also served as the estate of George Alfred Townsend, a twenty-something correspondent during the war for the *New York Herald*. Between 1885 and 1914, Townsend peppered the landscape with buildings, few of which remain. The most lasting memory of his estate is the War Correspondents Memorial that is situated at the intersection of Gapland Road and Arnoldstown Road. Its unique design matches its unique purpose, which was expanded from a tribute to Civil War reporters originally to, in 2003, a salute to American correspondents who died in any war. The monument, brought under the wing of the then War Department in 1904 and now maintained by the National Park Service, was built in 1896 with $5,500 in funds raised among friends.

Civil War Correspondents Memorial at Gathland State Park. (Photo by Leanna Joyner)

The names of 157 war reporters, artists, and photographers that documented the war are inscribed on tablets inset on the monument. The three arches along the top are said to represent description, depiction, and photography.

Townsend reported from front lines in 1862 for the Peninsular Campaign and again for the last several months of the war. He was a young journalist who covered the war with an eye for detail and the human interest of its soldiers and citizens.[262] After the war, he continued to write as a political columnist and investigative reporter. Among other topics, he investigated Lincoln's assassination. Townsend gained popularity and wealth as a newsman. Living comfortably from his earnings as "Gath," a pseudonym he adopted, he pursued more creative pursuits, including fiction and poetry.[263]

Townsend's first visit to Crampton Gap was in 1884, when he took a buggy ride from Harpers Ferry. Upon seeing the area, he purchased property for an estate he dubbed "Gapland."[264] One of the few buildings that remains serves as a museum where visitors can explore Gath's life and the local history. A self-guided tour of Gathland State Park includes interpretive signs, a visit to his mausoleum, and history of Gath and the estate.

Crampton Gap to Brownsville Gap Hike

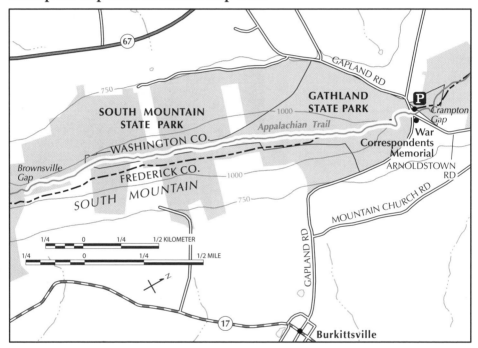

Distance: 3.4 miles
Difficulty: Easy
Trailhead directions: Arrive at Gathland State Park on Gapland Road, which intersects with Md. 67 on the western side of the ridge and Md. 17 in the middle of Burkittsville on the eastern side. The War Correspondents Memorial is on the northeast intersection of Gapland Road and Arnoldstown Road. Turn north on Arnoldstown Road, and drive a short distance to the parking area on the western side of the street. The parking lot is adjacent to a picnic pavilion on the northwest side of the intersection. If this lot is full, return to the intersection, and enter through the park gate to locate additional space near the museum.
Description: Begin this hike at the War Correspondents Memorial among informational displays on the northwestern, northeastern, and southern sides of Gapland Road. Please use caution while crossing the road. When you are ready, locate the Appalachian Trail blaze near the park gate on the southern side of Gapland.

Gathland State Park. (Photo by Acroterion, licensed under Creative Commons)

On your way through this section of the park, you will pass public restrooms on your right and the museum on your left. The Appalachian Trail continues into the woods between the museum and the mausoleum, indicated by a sign detailing distances to locations to the south. Follow the trail as it curves right and climbs slightly. Pass a path to the mausoleum on your right; you can take it on the return portion of this hike.

In less than 0.1 mile, a trail on your left leads to earthworks prepared for the defense of Crampton Gap. Once you've explored that short side trail, return to travel south on the A.T. The terrain of this section is remarkably easy to walk. Notice the rocks and boulders on your right that would have prevented an attack on the ridge anywhere but at the gaps. The Trail gently gains elevation before dropping slightly toward Brownsville Gap. You will pass one faint old road but continue on another 0.1 or 0.3 mile to reach a powerline cut across the ridge. This is Brownsville Gap. The visibility afforded by the powerline cut gives you a glimpse west to Pleasant Valley, where McLaws' troops bluffed the Union's Franklin into reconsidering his orders. On the eastern side of the ridge is Burkittsville, although a clear view of the town is difficult to acquire most times of the year.

Now that you've covered the line of the Confederate defense of Crampton Gap, return to Gathland Park the way you arrived.

Other Activities: Enthusiastic hikers may opt to walk the distance from Gathland State Park to Turners Gap, a seven-mile hike, by arranging for a shuttle pick-up at the South Mountain Inn at Turners Gap. Also nearby by vehicle are the Antietam National Battlefield and the Kennedy farm, used by John Brown for the final planning and arms-gathering before his attack on Harpers Ferry.

Fox Gap and Turners Gap

Fox Gap is one mile south along the ridge from Turners Gap. When General Robert E. Lee assigned General D.H. Hill (no relation to fellow Rebel General A.P. Hill) to hold the pass at Turners Gap, Hill expanded his right flank to reach Fox Gap. The Mountain House, now called the South Mountain Inn, served as Hill's headquarters. From his command on the ridgeline, he watched the long lines of blue-clad soldiers approach. With awe, Hill later described it as "a grand and glorious spectacle" that was "impossible to look at it without admiration." He continued, "I had never seen so tremendous an army before, and I did not see one like it afterward."[265]

Hill informed Lee of the Union columns approaching South Mountain with un-usual haste. Lee ordered General James Longstreet's command to march the twelve miles from Hagerstown to South Moun-tain in support of Hill's division, but Long-street's men didn't arrive at the gaps until 4 in the afternoon. Even with reinforce-ments, Hill's forces only numbered 14,000, opposed to the 28,000 Union soldiers who fought at Fox and Turners gaps that day.[266]

Fighting on September 14 began at 9 a.m. at Fox Gap as Union soldiers began to crest this sway in the ridge. They were met with shots fired from North Carolinians under General Samuel Garland, Jr. Reacting swiftly and with superior numbers, the Union returned fire and advanced. By midmorning, Garland was killed. Without their leader, the North Carolina bri-gade broke and ran toward the western valley.

During the battle at Fox Gap, Colonel Rutherford B. Hayes was shot in his left arm. This is Hayes' third appearance in Civil War history along the Appalachian Trail. He and members of his 23rd Ohio regiment had captured and held Pearisburg, Virginia, for several days in May of 1862. (See pages 35-39.) As he has been since Virginia, Hayes was still serving at this battle with future president William McKinley. After an election that had to be resolved by Congress, Hayes was inaugurated as the 19th presi-dent of the United States in 1877, succeeding Ulysses S. Grant. He served one term. McKinley died in office of an assassin's bullet 39 years to the day after the Fox Gap battle.

Having scattered the Confederates, the gap was briefly secured by General Jacob D. Cox's brigade. Cox considered leading his men north, along the present-day Appalachian Trail, to Turners Gap. Hill had acted quickly with his limited re-sources to erect a façade of a grand army positioned at the Mountain House with its cannons and guns directed to the south at Cox. In the face of the ruse, Cox held Fox Gap without advancing on the line of dismounted staff officers, couriers, teamsters, and cooks that he could have easily broken through.[267]

The Reno Monument, erected in 1889 by fellow soldiers at the top of Fox Gap along Reno Monument Road, commemorates the death of Union General Jesse L. Reno. (Photo by Leanna Joyner)

Stalled and awaiting reinforcements, the Union in Fox Gap was hit by a second wave of Confederates, led by G.B. Anderson. As fighting continued late into the afternoon, Federal reinforcements arrived. With fresh fighters from General Jesse L. Reno's IX Corps, the Union persisted in its control of the gap by rebuffing the attacks of Anderson and later Brigadier General Thomas F. Drayton's brigade. Around 4 p.m., outnumbered and desperate, rather than retreat, Confederate soldiers pushed hard against the Union line, then jumped behind stone walls to continue firing. Reno's troops advanced toward the stone walls to kill and capture the attackers. The Confederate lines broke and fell back once more. Feeling that the area was sufficiently secured, Reno rode forward to assess the situation at Turners Gap. On his scouting mission, he met the fourth wave of Confederate fighters sent to delay movement from the gap. A shot fired from General John Bell Hood's Texas Brigade wounded Reno, who died upon his return to Union lines. Fighting between Hood's and Reno's forces continued until nightfall.

Meanwhile, at Turners Gap, activity picked up as the afternoon progressed toward evening. By 4 p.m., Union General Joseph Hooker had regiments ready for an attack on the gap and to its north, and, on the other side, Longstreet's forces had arrived in support of Hill. Along the National Road (Alternate U.S. 40 today) through Turners Gap, Confederates under Alfred H. Colquitt had taken up strong defensive positions behind stone walls to resist the onslaught of General John Gibbon's Union forces. Methodically and tenaciously, the Iron Brigade under Gibbons advanced on the gap, meeting the fire of Southerners from behind logs, fences, rocks, and bushes to force them out of the woods.[268] They fought through dusk and into the night.

Just north of Turners Gap, Confederate General Robert E. Rhodes [a.k.a. Rodes] fought against the overwhelming odds presented by Hooker's corps. Fighting raged between them until late in the evening.[269] At 11 p.m., Lee called all of his regiments back from Fox and Turners gaps to regroup at Sharpsburg, a small town along Antietam Creek nine miles away, and await unification with troops from Crampton Gap and those returning from the siege of Harpers Ferry. Confederate casualties at Fox and Turners gaps were between 1,900 and 2,700 men. The Union loss was nearly as much, with 1,813 casualties recorded.[270]

Dahlgren Chapel at Turners Gap. (Photo by Leanna Joyner)

Perhaps the most gruesome story from the Fox Gap battle to be passed on to the next centuries was that, two days after the battle, Union burial details from the late General Reno's command dumped 58 Rebels' bodies down farmer Daniel Wise's well, northwest of the current monument at the gap. Federal soldiers had slept the night before next to the bodies of dead Confederates clustered around the stone fence that had served as their defense line. An unnamed North Carolinian died while crossing the stone fence and stiffened still straddled across it with his arms outstretched and mouth open.[271] Twelve years later, the remains were retrieved by black laborers, put two to a coffin box at the rate of $1.65 per skull, and buried at the new Confederate Cemetery in nearby Hagerstown.

Four years before the recovery of the bodies from the well, Maryland's governor had commissioned a survey of the locations of Rebel remains at the three Maryland battlefields (Antietam, South Mountain, and Monacy). It identified 758 soldiers but also determined the sites of another 2,481 who could not be identified; of the total, about 500 had been hastily buried on South Mountain. A half-century later, farmers in the valley battlefields continued to occasionally plow up troops' bones.[272]

Turners Gap Hike

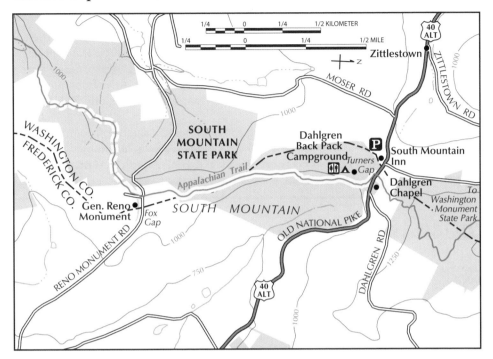

Distance: 2.2 miles

Difficulty: Easy

Trailhead directions: Park on the southern side of Alternate U.S. 40 in the space designated as A.T. trailhead parking below South Mountain Inn.

Description: From the parking area, cross U.S. 40-A toward tablets commemorating the Battle of South Mountain and interpretive signs about the National Road. Stay on this side of the road, and follow the Appalachian Trail north a short distance to pass to the right of an old apple tree and to the left and behind Dahlgren Chapel. Before the trail disappears into the woods, you have an excellent vantage point to view the valley to the east. It would have been from a perspective similar to this that Confederate D.H. Hill looked east and saw Union soldiers for "as far as the eye can see." With this imposing thought, turn back toward South Mountain Inn, and hike south on the A.T., crossing back over U.S. 40-A.

The trail quickly disappears into the woods beside the road and parallels a gated maintenance road. In 0.2 mile, pass the Dahlgren Back Pack Campground on your right; public restrooms are available here between April and October. Continue south on the trail on a wide footpath that feels distinctly like an old woods road, which it was as far back as the Civil War. The trail ambles easily along the wooded crest, then follows the edge of a field to reach Reno Monument Road 1 mile in to your hike. Interpretive signs and commemorative plaques are easily found in the area. Just east of the Trail crossing is a monument honoring General Reno.

Hikers can turn back now to return to Turners Gap or explore the battleground of

Fox Gap further by continuing south on the A.T. for another 0.75 mile to an unmarked field where the battle at Fox Gap on September 14 began. The North Carolinians lost so much ground within the first few hours of fighting that much of the rest of the battle occurred closer to Fox Gap. Conclude the walk by hiking back north on the A.T. to return to the parking area.

Other Activities: Pay homage to America's first president and discover the Civil War-era significance of the Washington Monument. The monument is a short drive from Turners Gap or a 1.8-mile hike north on the A.T. See below.

The Antietam National Battlefield around Sharpsburg is a short drive from Boonsboro (2.3 miles west on U.S. 40-A) and offers many opportunities to explore Civil War history beyond South Mountain.

For those who want to continue exploring South Mountain and the Appalachian Trail, consider a visit to Greenbrier State Park for hiking, paddling, camping, or bicycling. It is a few miles north of Boonsboro by car and about five miles north of Turners Gap on the trail by foot.

The Washington Monument

The cylindrical Washington Monument was the first tribute of its kind to George Washington. Erected in 1827 and restored in 1936, the monument served as a viewing platform and signal station several times during the Civil War. Citizens of Boonsboro were first to use it as an observation point when they climbed the tower to see the Battle of South Mountain, all around them to the south, on Sep-

tember 14, 1862. Later, it was used by Union troops during the Battle of Antietam/Sharpsburg a few days later, during Confederate General J.E.B. Stuart's raid into Pennsylvania in October 1862, and in 1863 during Robert E. Lee's withdrawal from Gettysburg. A museum near the monument details the structure's history and Civil War importance.

The first monument to George Washington also served as an observation point on several occasions during the Civil War. Today hikers can still climb the interior stone spiral staircase to gain a view of Boonsboro and Pleasant Valley. (Photo by Leanna Joyner)

Washington Monument Exploration Hike

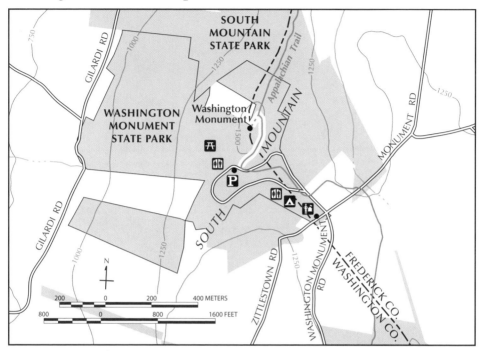

Distance: 0.3 mile

Difficulty: Easy

Directions: From Alternate U.S. 40, turn onto Washington Monument Road, also indicated by signs for Washington Monument State Park. Travel 0.9 mile to an intersection with Zittlestown Road. Proceed through the stop sign to enter Washington Monument State Park. A $3 entrance fee is assessed per vehicle at a self-service station at the park entrance. In 0.1 mile, reach the first of three available parking lots.

Description: This is an enjoyable hike for all ages. It offers easy terrain and rewarding views from the monument. The hike begins near the museum building and a trailside kiosk. For the next 0.1 mile, this access trail is aligned with the Appalachian Trail. The A.T. turns off to the right, indicated by double white blazes on trees, but visitors to the monument stay on the wide path to swing left within sight of the monument.

If you climb the stairs to the top of the tower or observe Boonsboro from the platform, you can see how this would make an excellent signal station. Looking down on Boonsboro, you can also imagine the battle that was fought there following the Battle of Gettysburg.

More information about the trail in this area, along with more history of nearby points, can be found in the *Appalachian Trail Guide to Maryland–Northern Virginia*, available at the Ultimate Appalachian Trail Store˚ (*www.atctrailstore.org*).

Battle of Gettysburg, from a Stereograph by E.W. Kelley, Chicago, 1897. (Library of Congress)

Before and After the Battle of Gettysburg

June and July 1863 brought another invasion of the North by Robert E. Lee's Army of Northern Virginia. The Southerners again had their aim set at capturing Harrisburg, since it served a strategic role as a supply hub for the Union. The Pennsylvania Railroad through that capital city was thought to have transported as many as 750,000 Federal troops during the course of the war.[273] As the U.S. Army advanced protectively toward Harrisburg, Lee altered his commands to convene forces at Gettysburg.

The Battle of Gettysburg, perhaps the most well-known of all Civil War battles, in which 51,000 people lost their lives in three days of fighting, was fought in and around of the town of that name just east of South Mountain.

The transportation of troops leading up to the battle and following the fight required movement over the ridge along which the Appalachian Trail now runs in Maryland and Pennsylvania. In some cases, the passes of the mountain in Maryland and Pennsylvania shaped the course of the fighting in Gettysburg. At its closest, the Appalachian Trail, where it crosses U.S. 30 and enters Caledonia State Park, is just thirteen miles from the battleground at Gettysburg. What is now U.S. 30 was also the most frequently used military route to the battle.

Gettysburg is also nineteen miles from the A.T. crossing at Mount Holly Springs and eighteen miles from Monterey Pass on present-day Pa. 16. The A.T. crossing at Pa. 16, slightly more than two miles into the Keystone State from the south, also traverses the site of a battle on July 4-5, the only skirmish to spill over onto both sides of the Mason–Dixon line.

As the Confederate forces moved toward Gettysburg, they frequently touched what became spots along the Appalachian Trail:

Virginia

The proximity of northern Virginia to Maryland required frequent passages over the gaps of the Blue Ridge both before and after the Battle of Gettysburg.

Ashby Gap—As Lee moved into Maryland, J.E.B. Stuart fell back to Ashby Gap on June 21 after "furious fighting" with Union cavalry in Upperville.[274]

Following their Gettysburg victory, Union troops took control of the gap on July 20, 1863.[275]

Snickers Gap—After leaving Culpeper, Confederate General Richard S. Ewell travelled north, then west over Snickers Gap to reach Berryville on June 13. He crossed into Maryland three days later.[276]

On June 28, Colonel John Mosby took fifty of his Partisan Rangers and crossed into Pennsylvania. Rather than merging with the remainder of Lee's forces at Gettysburg, Mosby's men returned to northern Virginia in three days with 218 cattle, fifty horses, and twelve blacks captured as escaped slaves.[277]

Maryland

Southerners stayed to the west of South Mountain as they entered Pennsylvania in June 1863. Federals took up positions along the ridge to watch their progress and return information on their movements to General Joseph Hooker. The more significant activity occurred on Lee's retreat from Gettysburg, followed closely by General George G. Meade's men, which resulted in the Battle of Boonsboro just a few miles from South Mountain's Turners Gap.

Crampton Gap—As early as June 18, Union General Hooker had established an observation and signal station at the gap.[278] Federals retained control of this gap through the course of the battle at Gettysburg.

Turners Gap—For the duration of the Southern invasion in the summer of 1863, Federals took up a position at the Mountain House at Turners Gap. Previously, Confederate and Union troops used it for the battles of South Mountain and Antietam, respectively.[279]

As the summer wore on, signal stations at Turners Gap, at Crampton Gap, and at the Washington Monument were a vital tool for Union officers to communicate Southern troop movements.

As Lee's troops filtered into Maryland on their retreat from Gettysburg, they populated Pleasant Valley to the west below South Mountain. Stalled on their retreat by the high waters of the Potomac, Confederate cavalry under General J.E.B. Stuart was ordered to stave off encroaching Union cavalry under General Alfred Pleasonton. The resulting July 8 Battle of Boonsboro was a cavalry battle—fought, unlikely enough, dismounted and from behind the cover provided by trees, stone walls, and fences, since the extremely muddy ground made a charge on horseback impossible.[280]

Gettysburg National Military Park. View looking east across The Wheatfield at Little Round Top (left) and Big Round Top. (Photo by David T. Gilbert)

By July 9, as Meade's army closed in on Lee's forces, stranded by the flooded Potomac, he took over the Mountain House as Union headquarters.

Pennsylvania

Most of Lee's Gettysburg-bound Army of Northern Virginia was in Pennsylvania by June 28. Some were as far north as the outskirts of Harrisburg, some were as far west as Chambersburg, and others were as far east as York when orders were issued to march to Gettysburg. The troops arriving from the north and west were limited to using two passes in South Mountain: Cashtown Pass and a route through Mount Holly Springs.

On their retreat, Lee's forces again used Cashtown Pass, on what was also known as Chambersburg Pike, and a pass to the south known as Monterey Pass. A skirmish had occurred in that area on June 22 between Virginia cavalry and Pennsylvania cavalry. Almost two weeks later, Confederates used this pass as the shortest route back to Maryland.

When the Battle of Gettysburg drew to a close on Friday afternoon, July 3, Lee's troops were divided so that the bulk of the forces traveled south on the eastern side of the ridge to then pass through Monterey Pass. The long wagon train of wounded soldiers and supplies led by Brigadier General John D. Imoden was routed through Cashtown Gap. In the driving rain, Confederates wedged themselves through the pass as quickly as the muddy, slippery roads would permit while they were nipped at the heels by Union troops, only to be devastated.[281]

Meade ordered Union cavalry led by General Judson Kilpatrick to attack and harass the retreating Confederates. Fighting that began in a thunderstorm on the evening of July 4 spilled over to the next day and resulted in the capture or destruction of nine miles of Confederate wagon trains. A historical marker near the Appalachian Trail says that Kilpatrick also captured 1,500 prisoners.[282] Historians point it out as the second largest Civil War struggle on Pennsylvania soil.

Mason–Dixon Line to Monterey Pass

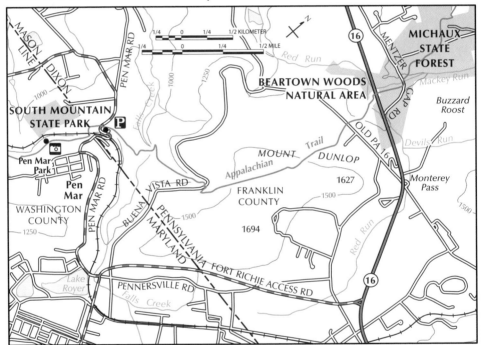

Distance: 5.7 miles

Difficulty: Moderate

Trailhead directions: From I-81, take Pa. 16 east to Rouzerville, Pa. In Rouzerville, turn right onto Pen Mar Road. The A.T. crosses Pen Mar Road 90 yards before a bridge over railroad tracks. On the left side of the road is room for two cars to park.

Description: From that shoulder parking area, you are 0.1 mile north of the Mason-Dixon line and 0.3 mile north of the dance pavilion and overlook shelter in Maryland's Pen Mar Park. To begin this hike, walk south on the A.T. to cross the A.T. corridor gate and shortly cross railroad tracks to walk uphill along a gravel lane. In 0.2 mile, enter a grassy area. An overlook shelter to the west, right, offers views, and the dance pavilion is to the east. Both offer shelter and perspectives on the landscape.

Return to Pen Mar Road the way you came, crossing the Mason-Dixon line from the south this time, approaching it with the significance felt by escaped slaves on the Underground Railroad, who, in pursuit of freedom, took a monumental step toward independence once they reached the free-state soil of Pennsylvania. Albeit symbolic, the boundary of Southern and Northern states in the war was drawn at this place; by crossing this line, General Lee threatened, more than ever, the security of the Union. (The Mason-Dixon line was established in 1765 to mediate a dispute between Great Britain and the American colonies and has served ever since as the boundary between Pennsylvania and Maryland.)

Cross into Pennsylvania, and soon follow the white blazes into the woods on the left, leaving the powerline right-of-way behind. In 0.3 mile, reach an old trolley line (used to carry visitors to Pen Mar Park) and an old stone wall. Cross Falls Creek on a footbridge in 0.2 mile, then cross Buena Vista Road in another 0.4 mile. Enter Michaux State Forest, and cross a log bridge over Red Run. Soon, you will cross over Old Pa. 16. Continue on just 0.3 mile farther to Pa. 16 and Monterey Pass.

Just west of the A.T. crossing of Pa. 16 is a township park dedicated to the Battle of Monterey Pass. The 2.6 miles you have walked from the Mason-Dixon line to this gap spans the territory through which the skirmish noted above between Union cavalry and retreating Confederate wagon trains was fought.

Return to your vehicle by retracing your steps south along the A.T. to Pen Mar Road.

Caledonia Iron Works and Caledonia State Park

The Appalachian Trail enters Caledonia State Park and skirts along the perimeter of the park's boundary with U.S. 30 to travel in the footsteps of thousands of soldiers who passed through this area between June 28 and July 5, 1863.

The present-day park was once the site of an iron furnace and related works owned by abolitionist and legislator Thaddeus Stevens (see page 5). Built in 1837, it was burned on June 23, 1863, by Confederate General Jubal A. Early *en route* to Gettysburg, in an effort to stem the flow of iron for weapons production for the North as much as to personally protest Stevens' vocal and unwavering feelings on abolition.

Following the looting and arson of the iron works, Early traveled east to York. In a few more days, the road in front of Caledonia became a major thoroughfare for A.P. Hill's troops, followed by James Longstreet's regiments traveling from Chambersburg to Gettysburg. In fact, so many troops were trying to move through the narrow pass that a bottleneck developed. The problem was compounded when Richard S. Ewell's troops from Mount Holly Springs joined the procession toward Gettysburg on the eastern side of the ridge.[283] An Appalachian Trail guide from 1974 said that, on July 1, Longstreet was delayed by at least six hours due to the constriction at the pass and that the first of his troops did not reach the vicinity of Gettysburg until after dark.[284]

Caledonia State Park Hike

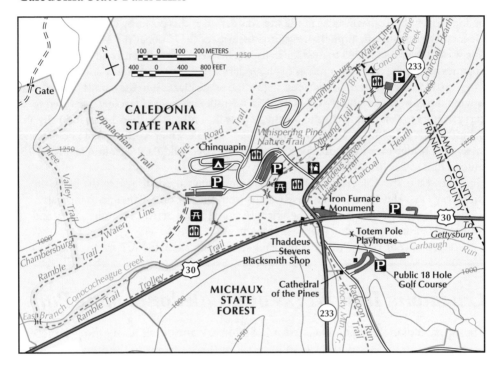

Distance: 1.45 miles

Trailhead directions: Arrive at Caledonia State Park by taking the exit for U.S. 30 off I-81. Travel east on U.S. 30 for 10 miles. At the intersection with Pa. 233, turn left, passing a parking area on your right at an iron-furnace monument. Continue on Pa. 233 another 0.1 mile, and the entrance to the park is on your left. Beyond the ranger station and information center, the road passes one parking lot on the left and continues past the entrance to Chinquapin Hill camping area and near the swimming pool. The trailhead parking lot is the next left.

Description: From the trailhead parking lot, the Appalachian Trail passes just beyond the picnic tables of this day-use area. Proceed on the Appalachian Trail south toward the playground and in the direction of U.S. 30. The Trail parallels Conococheague Creek for a short distance and intersects with the Ramble Trail. Rather than proceed on the A.T. farther south across U.S. 30, take the right fork of the junction, and continue to parallel the creek, crossing over two small bridges. The Ramble Trail intersects the Three Valley Trail, and hikers wishing to extend this hike another half-mile can follow this northward trail to its intersection with the A.T., where they can turn right and return to the parking area. Otherwise, to remain on this loop, follow the Ramble Trail to its junction with the Chambersburg Water Line, a hiking path, and turn right to follow the line on a direct route back to the picnic and parking area.

Other Activities: Visitors interested in exploring the rich history of iron production will find interpretive exhibits and information at the blacksmith shop and the iron-furnace monument. Energetic hikers may chose to take a longer hike to explore the charcoal hearths on the Charcoal Hearth and Thaddeus Stevens Trail Loop; this hike begins at the iron-furnace monument. The swimming pool and playground offer respite for younger hikers, and the Totem Pole Playhouse offers entertainment in the summer months. Thirteen miles east is the historic town of Gettysburg. The drive on U.S. 30 echoes the path that Early, Hill, and Longstreet took on their way to the famous battle. Visitors may choose to take a short drive 10 miles west to Chambersburg (on I-81) to visit the earlier farmhouse used by John Brown at 225 East King Street, where Brown lived while preparing for his raid on Harpers Ferry, before moving to the Kennedy farm in Maryland.

Mount Holly Springs/Pa. 34

Confederate General Richard Ewell's troops had reached the outskirts of Harrisburg overlooking the Susquehanna River when he received orders to return by way of Mount Holly Springs and Heidelsburg to Gettysburg. With 40,000 troops, Ewell moved through the gap just a mile from the town of Mount Holly Springs.[285] The grave of an unknown Confederate soldier who fell ill on the march is marked in a cemetery here. Employees at a circa-1810 inn then known as the Mullin Hotel had been ordered by Ewell to nurse his unidentified, ill, teen-aged soldier back to health, but he succumbed after several days of treatment and prayer.[286]

Susquehanna River

The Appalachian Trail crosses the Susquehanna River near Duncannon, fifteen miles upstream from Harrisburg. Attacks on Harrisburg had been planned for September 1862 and again in July 1863, but they were never consummated. The Confederate army under Ewell halted its advance to Harrisburg just a few miles outside it on June 28 when Lee called soldiers to Gettysburg. (A.T. hikers can achieve a bird's-eye view of the wide Susquehanna River from atop Hawk Rock, a strenuous 2.2-mile hike up from the town of Duncannon, although it is far removed from any Civil War activity.)

More information about the trail in this area, along with more history of nearby points, can be found in the *Appalachian Trail Guide to Maryland–Northern Virginia* and the *Appalachian Trail Guide to Pennsylvania,* available at the Ultimate Appalachian Trail Store* (*www.atctrailstore.org*).

"Arrival of freedmen and their families at Baltimore, Maryland—an every day scene" by Frank
Leslie, New York, September 30, 1865. (Library of Congress)

Post-War Period

Freed Slaves' Community at Brown Mountain Creek

A short distance south of the town of Buena Vista in central Virginia, where the Appalachian Trail passes through a fairly narrow valley, the land around Brown Mountain Creek was home to families, cabins, animals, and fields of crops—a hollow with a history of slavery as well as freedom for African-Americans after the Civil War.

In antebellum Amherst County, Jesse Richeson owned a plantation of 2,000 acres, farmed by slave labor, producing corn and tobacco.[287] His property included part of Brown Mountain Creek. He had a son, Mose, by one of his slaves. Mose was a slave but was allowed to work in a mill owned by his father to earn money. It was through this circumstance that Mose had the resources to purchase 220 acres of property at Brown Mountain Creek three years after the war. That purchase made him one of the few freed slaves in Appalachia to own land. Furthermore, as his wealth increased, he became one of the largest landowners in the area. He and his sons eventually acquired about 700 acres.[288]

Mose Richeson rented property and cabins to other former slaves, who sharecropped the land. At least eleven families lived in this freed-slaves community at the turn of the twentieth century.[289] Residents grew tobacco, corn, oats, and wheat on the terraced slopes. They collected persimmons, apples, and chestnuts from the trees. A former resident, Taft Hughes, said his family raised chickens, kept a team of horses to use on the fields, and had one cow for milk.[290] A grist mill owned and operated in the village ground grain and corn. Higher on the hill was the community cemetery.[291]

A walk today along the A.T. passes hidden clues of those who lived and worked here. The stories of the past are obscured with the thick canopy of reforested woodlands and the slowly diminishing evidence of their homes and barns. However, a careful look reveals rock walls and foundations.

Brown Mountain Loop Hike

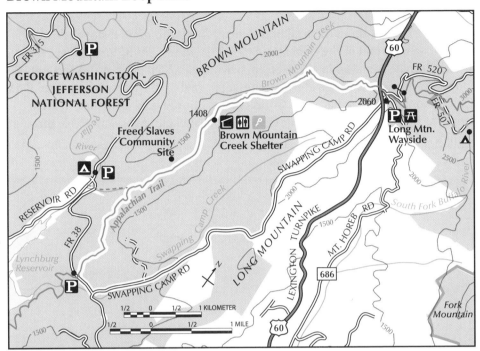

Distance: 7.2 miles

Difficulty: Moderate

Trailhead directions: From Buena Vista, Virginia, travel east on U.S. 60 for 9.3 miles to reach Long Mountain Wayside and a trailhead parking area with picnic tables, grills, and garbage cans.

Description: This hike begins with a southbound walk on the Appalachian Trail. Locate the trail from the parking area by crossing the highway on a right diagonal. Descend log steps, and soon cross over a small branch of Brown Mountain Creek. In 1.1 mile, reach an interpretive sign about the history of sharecroppers in the area. Walk with the intention of observing all of the remnants of cabins, barns, and spring boxes. Remember that all visitors can experience the archaeology and history of this place when they are observed from a distance. Take pictures or draw pictures to remember your visit here, but *please refrain from climbing on or moving hand-stacked rocks in this area.*

In 0.7 mile, the trail comes to the Brown Mountain Creek Shelter, which sleeps six and has a picnic table and a privy. The trail south of here crosses the creek on a lovely bridge and continues to kindle the imagination about the lives lived in this valley in the wake of four years of war. In 0.8 mile, hikers encounter another sign on the history of the area and a bench. In another 0.8 mile, cross an old logging road, and then cross a small stream. In a half-mile, reach the junction with a gravel Forest Service road, labeled No. 38 on A.T. maps and also called Swapping Camp Road. Turn left on the gravel road, and ascend the 3.4 miles back to U.S. 60.

If you want to see the history of Brown Mountain Creek in a different way, you can also hike back the way you came, because everything along a trail looks changed given an opposite perspective. Returning the way you came makes for a total distance of 7.6 miles.

More information about the trail in this area, along with more history of nearby points, can be found in the *Appalachian Trail Guide to Central Virginia,* available at the Ultimate Appalachian Trail Store˚ (*www.atctrailstore.org*). A full account of Jodi A. Barnes' archaeological work here, supported by the Appalachian Trail Park Office and the Appalachian Trail Conservancy, is more fully described in *From Farms to Forests: The Material Life of an Appalachian Landscape,* available through Google Books.

Chronology of Events in this Guide

1850s–1860s—Underground Railroad.

1859
October 15–18—John Brown's raid on Harpers Ferry, Virginia.

1861
April 18—Federals burn arsenal on retreat from Harpers Ferry.
July 19–20—Confederate General Stonewall Jackson's men overnight at Ashby
    Gap, Virginia, before engaging at first Battle of Manassas/Bull Run.

1862
May—Stonewall Jackson passes through Browns Gap and Rockfish Gap, Virginia,
    as part of the Shenandoah Valley campaign.
May—Confederate General Richard S. Ewell camps with 8,000 troops at Swift Run
    Gap before joining Jackson in Shenandoah Valley campaign.
May 6–10—Union occupation of Pearisburg, Virginia.
May 15—Union wagon train attacked in Manassas Gap, Virginia.
September 14—Battle of South Mountain, Maryland.
September 15—Confederate siege of Harpers Ferry.
November—Skirmish in Manassas Gap.

1863
January—Establishment of John S. Mosby's Rangers in northern Virginia.
May 5—Attempt by Union to capture Mosby in Snickers Gap, Virginia.
June 22—Skirmish at Monterey Pass (Pa. 16).
June 23—Confederate General Jubal A. Early burns Caledonia Iron Works, Penn-
    sylvania.
July 4–5—Fighting at Monterey Pass, capture of Confederate wagons and prison-
    ers.
July 8—Battle of Boonsboro, Maryland.
July 21, 23—Skirmishes at Manassas Gap.
July 22—Chester Gap, Virginia.
October 20, 23, 26—Skirmishes in Hot Springs, North Carolina.
November 26, 1863—More skirmishes in Hot Springs.

1864

January—Shelton Laurel Massacre in Tennessee.

January 10—Mosby's attack on Federal cavalry at Loudoun Heights, Virginia.

May 6, 10–11—Union General George Crook crosses the future A.T. at two points in southwest Virginia as part of a mission to destroy the Virginia railroad.

June 11—Virginia Military Institute cadets camp along James River near current A.T.

June 15—Confederates, followed by Federals, ascend Bearwallow Gap, Virginia, along the Blue Ridge crest.

July 16—Fight between General Early and General Crook at Snickers Gap.

July 19—Sheltons, near Big Butt in North Carolina, ambushed and killed.

July 19—Skirmishing at Ashby Gap.

September 15—Union attempt to capture Mosby's Rangers at Snickers Gap.

September 23—Mosby's men captured at Chester Gap and later executed in Front Royal under orders from General George A. Custer.

December 29—Battle of Red Banks (near Erwin, Tennessee).

1865

March 3—Battle of Waynesboro, Virginia, near Rockfish Gap.

April 8—Mosby passes through Ashby Gap on his last scouting mission as a Confederate Ranger.

1867—Establishment of Storer College, Harpers Ferry, West Virginia.

1868—Mose Richeson, a freed slave, purchases land from his former owner/father and establishes freed-black community in Amherst County, Virginia.

1891

John Brown's "fort" moved to Chicago.

1895

John Brown's "fort" moved to Murphy Farm, Harpers Ferry.

1906

Aug 15-19—Second Niagara Conference held at Storer College.

1909

John Browns "fort" moved to Storer College campus.

1968

John Brown's "fort" moved to within 150 feet of its original site in lower town Harpers Ferry.

Directory of Hikes

Use this south-to-north guide to identify a hike to suit your quest for historical sites of the Civil War and related eras.

All the A.T. maps listed here are available for purchase from the Ultimate Appalachian Trail Store* at *www.atctrailstore.org* or by calling (888) 287-8673 weekdays between 9 a.m. and 4:30 p.m. Eastern time.

Hike	Distance (miles)	Type	Difficulty	Historic Significance	A.T. Map
Lovers Leap Loop (page 24)	1.6	Loop	Easy	Union occupation of Warm Springs [Hot Springs], N.C.	ATC Tenn.–N.C. Map 4
Shelton Graves (page 31)	10.4	Out and back	Moderate	Union soldiers killed and interred	Tenn.–N.C. Map 3
Cliff Ridge (page 33)	3	Out and back	Moderate	Battle of Red Banks	Tenn.–N.C. Map 3
Angels Rest (page 36)	5	Out and back	Strenuous	Union occupation of Pearisburg, Va.	ATC Southwest Va. Map 1
Wind Rock (page 43)	0.5	Out and back	Easy	Mini Ball Hill	ATC Central Va. Map 4
McAfee Knob (page 52)	7.4	Out and back	Moderate	Retreat of Union forces following defeat at Lynchburg	ATC Central Va. Map 3
Peaks of Otter Overlook (page 53)	1.4	Out and back	Easy	Hunter's Raid in the Shenandoah Valley	ATC Central Va. Map 2
Brown Mountain Loop (page 141)	7.2	Loop	Moderate	Community of former slaves	ATC Central Va. Maps 1-2
Browns Gap (page 48)	4.8	Loop	Easy/ Moderate	Stonewall Jackson's passage to surprise and overtake Union forces in Shenandoah Valley	PATC Map 11

Hike	Distance (miles)	Type	Difficulty	Historic Significance	A.T. Map
Hightop Mountain (page 47)	3	Out and back	Strenuous	Perspective of Shenandoah Valley and encampment of Ewell's Confederate forces in Swift Run Gap during Shenandoah Valley Campaign of 1862	PATC Map 11
Mosby Campsite (page 64)	6	Out and back	Moderate	Land of "Mosby's Confederacy"	PATC Map 8
Ashby Gap and Signal Knob (page 68)	7.3	Out and back (with loop)	Easy/ Moderate	Jackson's encampment before First Battle of Manassas/ Bull Run. "Mosby's Confederacy"	PATC Map 8
Bears Den Rocks and Snickers Gap (page 73)	1.4	Loop	Easy	"Mosby's Confederacy"	PATC Map 8
Loudoun Heights (page 81)	4.6	Out and back	Moderate	Civil War activity 1861–1865	PATC Map 7
Camp Hill and A.T. Amble (page 99)	1.9	Loop	Easy	Civil War activity, 1861–1865; Storer College; Niagara Movement	PATC Map 7
Virginius Island and Lower Town Loop (page 102)	1.8	Loop	Easy	John Brown's Raid on Harpers Ferry and Civil War activity	PATC Map 7
Maryland Heights (page 105)	4.5 (or 6.5)	Out and back	Strenuous	Civil War activity	PATC Map 7
Crampton Gap to Brownsville Gap (page 122)	3.4	Out and back	Easy	National War Correspondents Memorial, Battle of South Mountain	PATC Map 5–6
Turners Gap to Fox/Reno Gaps (page 127)	2.2	Out and back	Easy	Battle of South Mountain	PATC Map 5–6
Washington Monument (page 129)	0.3	Out and back	Easy	Battle of South Mountain, Battle of Boonsboro	PATC Map 5–6

Hike	Distance (miles)	Type	Difficulty	Historic Significance	A.T. Map
Mason–Dixon Line to Monterey Pass (page 134)	5.7	Out and back	Moderate	Underground Railroad, general interest, Civil War skirmishes	PATC Map 4
Caledonia State Park Loop (page 8 or 136)	1.45	Loop	Easy	Underground Railroad, burning of iron works by Confederates	PATC Map 2–3 or map produced by Pa. Department of Natural Resources
Pine GroveFurnace (page 10)	1	Loop	Easy	Underground Railroad	PATC Map 2–3
Children's Lake (page 14)	0.7	Loop	Easy	Underground Railroad	PATC Map 1
Du Bois in Great Barrington (page 112)	10.2	Point-to-Point	Moderate	Civil Rights movement	Mass.–Conn. Maps 2 and 3

Footnotes

1   Siebert, Wilbur H. *The Underground Railroad from Slavery to Freedom* (2006 or original 1898), Macmillan, p. 33

2   Du Bois, W.E.B., *John Brown* (1909), G.W. Jacobs & Company, p. 120

3   Siebert, *op. cit.*, p. 54

4   *Appalachian Trail Guide to Maryland–Northern Virginia* (1989), Potomac Appalachian Trail Club (PATC)

5   Blockson, Charles L., *The Underground Railroad in Pennsylvania* (1981), Flame International, p. 144

6   *Appalachian Trail Guide to Maryland and Northern Virginia*, ninth edition (1974), PATC, p. 89

7   Switala, William J., *The Underground Railroad in Delaware, Maryland and West Virginia* (2004), Stackpole Books, pp. 101-102

8   *Ibid*, p. 101

9   Blockson, *op. cit.*, p. 146. (A quotation from "conductor" Hiriam Wertz, who stated he was familiar with every station along the historical South Mountain and Antietam route, from the Potomac River along South Mountain to the Pennsylvania border, said, "The first station in Pennsylvania was known as Shockey's. It was near the present village of Rouzerville, at the mountain's foot.")

10 *Ibid*

11 www.hallowedground.org/content/view/468/

12 Switala, *The Underground Railroad in Pennsylvania,* second edition (2008), p. 107

13 Siebert, *op. cit.*

14 Switala, *The Underground Railroad in Pennsylvania,* p. 107

15 *Ibid*, p. 108-111

16 Tritt, Richard L., *At a Place Called Boiling Springs* (1995), Sesquicentennial Committee, p. 115

17 *Ibid*

18 *Ibid*, p. 63

19 www.livingplaces.com/Pa./Cumberland_County/South_Middleton_Township/ Boiling_Springs_Historic_District.html

20 Switala, *The Underground Railroad in Pennsylvania,* p. 158

21 *Ibid*

22 *Ibid*. Robert Brown's home at the corner of Braeside Avenue and East Brown Street.

23 Department of Conservation and Natural Resources, "Pennsylvania Recreational Guide for Caledonia State Park" (2008)

24 Tate, J.R., *Walkin' with the Ghost Whisperers: Lore and Legends of the Appalachian Trail* (2005), p. 258

25 Department of Conservation and Natural Resources, *op. cit.*

26 Tate, *op. cit.*, p. 260

27 www.afrolumens.org/ugrr/whoswho/hnames.html

28 Switala, *The Underground Railroad in Pennsylvania*, p. 107

29 Siebert, *op. cit.*, p. 106

30 Current, R.N., *Old Thad Stevens* (1942), cited by the *Guide to the Appalachian Trail: Susquehanna River to the Shenandoah National Park,* fifth edition (1960), PATC, pp. 26-27

31 *Ibid,* p. 21

32 *Ibid,* p. 22

33 Switala, *The Underground Railroad in Delaware, Maryland and West Virginia*, p. 88

34 Siebert, *op. cit.*, p. 142

35 *Ibid,* p. 126

36 Upper Housatonic Valley African American Heritage Trail

37 Siebert, *op. cit.*, p.131

38 *Ibid;* map insert, p. 112-113

39 *Ibid,* p. 133

40 *Ibid,* p. 81

41 *Official Guide to the Appalachian Trail in Tennessee and North Carolina*, fifth edition (1976), Appalachian Trail Conference, Harpers Ferry, West Virginia, p. 8-14

42 Inscoe, John C., and McKinney, Gordon B., *The Heart of Confederate Appalachia: Western North Carolina in the Civil War* (2000), University of North Carolina Press, p. 89

43 *Ibid,* p. 16

44 *Ibid,* p. 89. Quotation of New York journalist Sidney Andrews, p. 91

45 *Ibid,* pg 54

46 Tipton, A. Christine, *Civil War in the Mountains: Greasy Cove, Tennessee* (2000), Shining Mountain Publishers, p. 2

47 Inscoe and McKinney, *op. cit.,* p. 114-115, and Tipton, *op. cit.,* p. 18

48 Inscoe and McKinney, *op. cit.,* p. 116-117

49 www.wtv-zone.com/civilwar/gkirk.html

50 www.nccivilwar150.com/timeline/chronology.htm

51 Inscoe and McKinney, *op. cit.,* p. 182

52 *Ibid,* p. 252

53 *Ibid,* p. 88

54 *Ibid,* p. 118

55 www.wncmagazine.com/feature/history/massacre_in_madison

56 Inscoe and McKinney, *op. cit.,* p. 119, and Tipton, *op. cit.,* p. 8

57 www.civilwar.nps.gov/cwss

58 Case of Elizabeth Shelton, Case No. 158257, National Archives, Washington. D.C.

59 *Ibid*

60 Tate, *op. cit.*, p. 96-97
61 www.civilwar.nps.gov/cwss
62 Tate, *op. cit.*, p. 97
63 *Ibid*
64 Case of Elizabeth Shelton, *op. cit.*
65 Tipton, *op. cit.*, p. 6
66 *Ibid*, p. 8
67 Hayes, Rutherford B., *Diary and Letters, Advance and Retreat 1862, Volume II* (1922), Ohio State Archaeological and Historical Society, p. 254
68 Hayes became president in a disputed election over Samuel Tilden. In the end, 20 Democratic electoral votes gave the election to Republican Hayes. Those votes came from three Southern states. Reconstruction "ended," and white supremacists resumed power there. Irony lived.
69 *Ibid*, p. 259
70 Whisonant, Robert, "Geology and the Civil War in Southwestern Virginia: Union Raiders in the New River Valley, May 1864," *Virginia Minerals,* November 1997, Vol. 43, No. 4, Virginia Department of Mines, Minerals and Energy, Richmond, p. 30
71 Marshall, C. Dale, "George Crook, The North's Most Overlooked General," *American Civil War*, November 1997, p. 41
72 Whisonant, *op. cit.*, p. 32, 39
73 *Ibid*, p. 36
74 Hayes, *op. cit.*, p. 257-258
75 *Appalachian Trail Guide to Central Virginia*, second edition (2010), Appalachian Trail Conservancy, p. 246
76 Hayes, *op. cit.*, p. 258
77 National Geographic Society, *Atlas of the Civil War* (2009), p. 68
78 Foote, Shelby, *The Civil War, a Narrative, Volume One: Fort Sumter to Perryville* (1958, revised 1986), Vintage Books, pp. 424-425
79 Swanston Publishing Limited, *The Atlas of the Civil War* (1994), pp. 66-67
80 *Ibid*, pp. 68-69
81 Duncan, Richard, (1998) *Lee's Endangered Left, The Civil War in Western Virginia, Spring 1864* (1998), LSU Press, pp. 230 and 250
82 *Ibid*, p. 221
83 *Ibid*, p. 232
84 *Ibid*, p. 252
85 *Ibid*, pp. 235-236, 240
86 Lynchburg, Virginia, museum exhibit (October 2010)
87 Duncan, *op. cit.*, Hastings diary entry from June 17, p. 246
88 American Documentaries, Inc., *The Civil War, an Illustrated History* (1990), p. 332
89 Swanston Publishing, *op. cit.*, pp. 168-171
90 Williamson, James J., *Mosby's Rangers* (1895), pp. 96-97

91 Mosby, John S., *The Memoirs of Colonel John S. Mosby* (1917), pp. 106-109

92 *Ibid*, pp. 119-120

93 National Geographic Society, *op. cit.*, pp. 84-87

94 Mosby, *op. cit.*, pp. 126-133

95 *Ibid*, pp. 148-150

96 Williamson, *op. cit.*, p. 26

97 Wert, Jeffery D., *Mosby's Rangers* (1990), p. 74

98 *Ibid*, p. 75

99 Williamson, *op. cit.*, p. 19

100 Wert, *op. cit.*, p. 157

101 Williamson, *op. cit.*, p. 175

102 Wert, *op. cit.*, p. 116

103 *Ibid*, p. 92

104 Williamson, *op. cit.*, p. 319

105 Williamson, *op. cit.*, p. 301, August 20 letter from Sheridan to Augur

106 Frye, Dennis, "Mosby as a Factor in the Campaign," *Struggle for the Shenandoah: Essays on the 1864 Valley Campaign* (1991), Kent State University Press, edited by Gary W. Gallagher, p. 108

107 Sam Moore as quoted in Wert, *op. cit.*, p. 193

108 Wert, *op. cit.*, p. 188

109 *The Union Army*, Volume 5, The American Civil War Research Database, Alexander Street Press, p. 273

110 Williamson, *op. cit.*, p. 239-240

111 *Ibid*

112 Wert, *op. cit.*, p. 223

113 Williamson, *op. cit.*, p. 175

114 *The Union Army*, Volume 6, *op. cit.*, p. 564

115 *Ibid*, p. 583

116 The American Civil War Research Database

117 Williamson, *op. cit.*, p. 171

118 *Guide to the Appalachian Trail: Susquehanna River to the Shenandoah National Park*, p. 209

119 *Appalachian Trail Guide to Maryland and Northern Virginia* (1974)

120 ranger95.com/civil_war/virginia/cavalry/rosters/43rd_cav_bn_rost_d_2.html

121 Tate, *op. cit.*, p. 184

122 Department of Historic Resources, 1996 historical marker

123 *The Union Army*, Volume 5, "Ashby's Gap, September 22, 1862"

124 www.civilwar.nps.gov/cwss/battles_trans.htm, and Williamson, *op. cit.*, p. 77

125 "Ashby's Gap, July 12-20, 1863," The American Civil War Research Database

126 Wert, *op. cit.*, Grant to Auger and Grant to Sheridan, p. 222

127 Williamson, *op. cit.*, report from General Duffié, p. 192-194

128 Wert, *op. cit.*, p. 245-250

129 Williamson, *op. cit.,* p. 299

130 *Ibid*

131 *Ibid,* p. 316

132 "Ashby's Gap, Feb. 19, 1865," The American Civil War Database; Williamson, *op. cit.,* pp. 343-351; Wert, *op. cit.,* p. 272

133 Williamson, *op. cit.,* p. 366

134 *Ibid,* p. 21

135 *Ibid,* pp. 62-63

136 *Ibid,* pp. 194-196, 202, 221

137 *Ibid,* p. 207; Wert, *op. cit.,* p. 190

138 Frye, *op. cit.,* pp. 114-115

139 *Ibid,* p. 114-115

140 Wert, *op. cit.,* p. 157

141 *Ibid,* pp. 205-207, 251-252

142 Mosby, *op. cit.,* pp. 298-300; Williamson, *op. cit.,* pp. 234-236

143 Mosby, *op. cit.,* pp. 300-301

144 Stover, John F., *History of the Baltimore and Ohio Railroad* (1995), Purdue University Press, p. 112

145 Wert, *op. cit.,* pp. 323-335

146 Frye, *op. cit.,* pp. 115-116

147 Williamson, *op. cit.,* p. 210)

148 Gilbert, David T., *A Walker's Guide to Harpers Ferry* (2008), Harpers Ferry Historical Association, p. 149

149 McPherson, James M., *Crossroads of Freedom: Antietam* (2002), Oxford University Press, p. 110; Bailey, Ronald H., *The Bloodiest Day* (1984), Time-Life Books, Inc., p. 39; historical tablets in Harpers Ferry National Historical Park

150 Harpers Ferry National Historical Park Civil War timeline

151 Wert, *op. cit.,* p. 134

152 Harpers Ferry National Historical Park Civil War timeline

153 Williamson, *op. cit.,* p. 131

154 Jones, *op. cit.,* pp. 170, 185, 240

155 Gilbert, *op. cit.,* pp. 146, 149

156 *Ibid,* p. 149

157 *Ibid,* pp. 150-151

158 *Ibid,* p. 39

159 U.S. Census Bureau Web site

160 Gilbert, *op. cit.,* p. 57

161 *Ibid,* pp. 146, 149

162 *Appalachian Trail Guide to Maryland and Northern Virginia* (1974), *op. cit.,* pp. 84-85; Harpers Ferry National Historical Park interpretive sign on Maryland Heights

163 Gilbert, *op. cit.,* p. 48

164 Du Bois, *op. cit.,* Frederick Douglas quoted by Du Bois, pp. 177-178

165 American Documentaries, Inc., *The Civil War: An Illustrated History* (1990), p. 2

166 Du Bois, *op. cit.*, p. 164

167 The 1860 Census documented that slaves made up half the population in Fauquier County.

168 Du Bois, *op. cit.*, p. 164

169 Du Bois, *op. cit.*, p. 133

170 Du Bois, *op. cit.*, Frederick Douglass as quoted by, p.133

171 Brown, John, *Provisional Constitution and Ordinances for the People of the United States* (1969), M&S Press, pp. 1-15; Du Bois, *op. cit.*, pp. 156-158

172 Gilbert, *op. cit.*, p. 44

173 Villard, *op. cit.*, p. 432; Du Bois, *op. cit.*, p. 187

174 Du Bois, *op. cit.*, p. 188

175 Villard, *op. cit.*, p. 432

176 Anderson, Osborne P., *A Voice from Harper's Ferry: A Narrative of Events at Harper's Ferry; with Incidents prior and subsequent to its capture by Captain Brown and his Men* (1861), p. 40

177 Villard, *op. cit.*, p. 427

178 *Ibid*, p. 438

179 *Ibid*, p. 441; Strain, Paula M., *The Blue Hills of Maryland: History along the Appalachian Trail on South Mountain and the Catoctins* (1993), Potomac Appalachian Trail Club, p. 10

180 Villard, *op. cit.*, p. 441; "John Brown's Raiders," produced by Harpers Ferry National Historical Park

181 Du Bois, *op. cit.*, Dangerfield as quoted in, p. 196

182 "John Brown's Raiders"

183 Strain, *op. cit.*, p. 9

184 Villard, *op. cit.*, p. 452

185 "John Brown's Raiders"

186 Du Bois, *op. cit.*, Brown as quoted in, p. 219

187 Gilbert, *op. cit.*, p. 41

188 Webster, Donald B., Jr., "The Last Days of Harpers Ferry Armory," *Civil War History*, Volume 5, No. 1, Kent State University Press, March 1959, p. 36

189 Gilbert, *op. cit.*, p. 40

190 Gilbert, *op. cit.*, p. 106

191 Webster, *op. cit.*, p. 42

192 docSouth.unc.edu/fpn/mosby/mosby.html; Mosby's Diary, page 29

193 Strain, *op. cit.*, p. 51; Gilbert, *op. cit.*, pp. 149-150,

194 Foote, *op. cit.*, p. 54

195 Harpers Ferry National Historical Park Civil War timeline

196 Mobley, E.C., *Georgia Weekly*, July 3, 1861

197 Gilbert, *op. cit.*, p. 48

198 Harpers Ferry National Historical Park Civil War timeline

199 *Ibid*; Gilbert, *op. cit.*, p. 137
200 Strain, *op. cit.*, p. 24; Foote, *op. cit.*, p. 680
201 *Ibid*, p. 21
202 McPherson, *op. cit.*, p. 109
203 Harpers Ferry National Historical Park Civil War timeline
204 *Ibid*
205 *Ibid*
206 Wert, *op. cit.*, pp. 131-132
207 Williamson, *op. cit.*, pp. 178-183
208 Harpers Ferry National Historical Park Civil War timeline
209 Hearn, Chester G., *Six Years in Hell: Harpers Ferry during the Civil War* (1996), p. 245-249
210 Gilbert, *op. cit.*, Jefferson as quoted in, p. 70
211 *Ibid*, p. 124
212 *Ibid*, pp. 47-48
213 Storer College Exhibit at Harpers Ferry National Historical Park (October 2010)
214 *Ibid*
215 www.wikipedia.com
216 Gilbert, *op. cit.*, p. 117-125
217 *Ibid*, p. 122
218 www.nps.gov/archive/hafe/storer.htm, accessed on February 23, 2011
219 *Ibid*
220 Niagara Movement Exhibit at Harpers Ferry National Historical Park (October 2010)
221 Gilbert, *op. cit.*, p. 126
222 Niagara Movement Exhibit
223 Black Voices Exhibit at Harpers Ferry National Historical Park (October 2010)
224 Niagara Movement Exhibit
225 www.nps.gov/archive/hafe/jbfort.htm, accessed on February 24, 2011
226 McVey, John, "John Brown's Fort Will be Heading Home," *The Journal*, Martinsburg, West Virginia (www.journal-news.net/page/category.detail/nav/5021, accessed on February 24, 2011)
227 Niagara Movement Exhibit
228 Quoted on www.Du Boisweb.org/greatbarrington.html
229 Southernberkshirechamber.com/faq
230 Foote, *op. cit.*, p. 662; McPherson, *op. cit.*, p. 56
231 McPherson, *op. cit.*, p. 94
232 *Ibid*, pp. 91-93
233 *Ibid*, p. 56
234 *Ibid*, p. 70
235 South Mountain Recreation Area Adventure Guide (2010), p. 10

236 McPherson, *op. cit.*, p. 89; Bailey, *op. cit.*, p. 18; American Documentaries, *op. cit.*, p. 151

237 Foote, *op. cit.*, p. 668

238 McPherson, *op. cit.*, p. 100, Bailey, *op. cit.*, p. 12, Foote, *op. cit.*, p. 663

239 Grove, S.E., *Souvenir and Guide Book of Harpers Ferry, Antietam and South Mountain Battlefield* (1905), Press of the Evening Globe, Hagerstown, p. 58

240 McPherson, *op. cit.*

241 Foote, *op. cit.*, p. 666; McPherson, *op. cit.*, p. 106; Maryland Civil War Trails, 1862 Antietam Campaign brochure; Bailey, *op. cit.*, p. 18

242 Foote, *op. cit.*, p. 668; Maryland Civil War Trails

243 The American Civil War Research Database, South Mountain, September 14, 1862

244 Maryland Civil War Trails

245 Foote, *op. cit.*, p. 670; Bailey, *op. cit.;* McPherson, *op. cit.*, p. 107, 108

246 McPherson, *op. cit.*, p. 107

247 American Documentaries, *op. cit.*, pp. 152-153; Foote, *op. cit.*, p. 672

248 Tate, *op. cit.*, p. 224-226

249 South Mountain Recreation Area Adventure Guide, p. 10

250 McPherson, *op. cit., New York World* as quoted by, p. 112

251 www.cr.nps.gov/hps/abp. /battles/md002.htm, accessed on January 31, 2011

252 *Ibid*

253 McPherson, *op. cit.*, p. 130

254 South Mountain Recreation Area Adventure Guide, p. 10

255 *Appalachian Trail Guide to Maryland and Northern Virginia* (1974), p. 89

256 Strain, *op. cit.*, p. 78

257 The American Civil War Research Database, South Mountain, Md.

258 McPherson, *op. cit.*, p. 111

259 Strain, *op. cit.*, p. 95

260 Bailey, *op. cit.*, p. 55

261 Foote, p. 680; Strain, *op. cit.*, p. 96

262 Shields, Jerry, *What Hath "Gath" Wrought,* jnjreid.com/cdb/townsend.html, accessed on February 1, 2011

263 *Ibid*

264 Strain, *op. cit.*, p. 101

265 Friends of South Mountain State Battlefield, www.friendsofsouthmountain. org/turnersgap, D.H. Hill as quoted by

266 McPherson, *op. cit.*, p. 111

267 Strain, *op. cit.*, pp. 132-133; Bailey, *op. cit.*, p. 47

268 Nolan, Alan T., *The Iron Brigade: A Military History* (1961), Indiana University Press, pp. 124-125

269 Bailey, *op. cit.*, p. 51

270 McPherson, *op. cit.*, p. 111

271 Swift, Robert, "The Political Express: Shadows over South Mountain," Sept. 4, 2012

272 *The Washington Times,* March 15, 2003

273 Author's Gettysburg-to-Harrisburg driving tour

274 www.civilwar.nps.gov/cwss/battles_trans.htm; Williamson, *op. cit.,* p. 77; Civil War Trails sign interpreting Battle of Upperville on U.S. 50

275 The American Civil War Research Database, "Ashby Gap, July 12-20, 1863"

276 Smith, Carl, *Gettysburg 1863: High Tide of the Confederacy,* Barnes and Noble Books, New York, 2000, p. 12-14

277 Williamson, *op. cit.,* pp. 79-80; Wert, *op. cit.,* p. 91

278 South Mountain Recreation Area Adventure Guide

279 *Ibid;* Strain, *op. cit.,* p. 145

280 Strain, *op. cit.,* p. 169

281 *Guide to the Appalachian Trail: Susquehanna River to the Shenandoah National Park,* fifth edition (1960), p. 25-25; Smith, *op. cit.,* p. 117

282 www.emmitsburg.net/montereypass/news

283 Trudeau, Noah Andre, *Gettysburg: A Testing of Courage* (2003), Harper Perennial, p. 133; *Guide to the Appalachian Trail: Susquehanna River to the Shenandoah National Park,* fifth edition (1960), pp. 23-24

284 *Appalachian Trail Guide to Maryland and Northern Virginia,* ninth edition, pp. 28-29

285 *Guide to the Appalachian Trail: Susquehanna River to the Shenandoah National Park,* fifth edition (1960), pp. 22, 24

286 Weaver, Frank, Jr., "Outtakes Around the Lakes: Ghosts Haunting the Holly Inn," published September 26, 2010, at www.thesuburbanite.com

287 Barnes, Jodi, "Wilderness: A Contemporary Archaeology of an Appalachia Landscape," The African Diaspora Archaeology Network newsletter, March 2008, p. 6

288 *Ibid,* p. 7

289 USDA Forest Service interview with Taft Hughes, nbatc.org/1992Interview

290 *Ibid*

291 *Ibid*

We are further indebted to the print and on-line publications of the Civil War Trust for facts, perspectives, and statistics, especially for the foreword.

Index